ILLUSTRATED ATLAS OF INDIA

Project editor Hina Jain
Editor Ayushi Thapliyal
US editor Karyn Gerhard
Editorial intern Sukriti Pandey
Project art editor Devika Awasthi
Art editor Priyal Mote
Map illustrator Arun Pottirayil
Illustrator Priyal Mote
Managing cartographer Suresh Kumar
Senior picture researcher Sumedha Chopra
Jacket designer Devika Awasthi
DTP designer Nand Kishor Acharya
Preproduction manager Narender Kumar
Managing editor Chitra Subramanyam
Managing art editor Neha Ahuja Chowdhry
Managing director, India Aparna Sharma

Subject expert Anusuya Roy

First American Edition, 2020
Published in the United States by DK Publishing
1450 Broadway, Suite 801, New York, NY 10018

Copyright © 2020 Dorling Kindersley Limited
DK, a Division of Penguin Random House LLC
20 21 22 23 24   10 9 8 7 6 5 4 3 2 1
001–322658–Nov/2020

All rights reserved.
Without limiting the rights under the copyright reserved above,
no part of this publication may be reproduced, stored in or
introduced into a retrieval system, or transmitted,
in any form, or by any means (electronic, mechanical,
photocopying, recording, or otherwise), without the
prior written permission of the copyright owner.
Published in India by Dorling Kindersley Limited

A catalog record for this book is available
from the Library of Congress.
ISBN 978-0-7440-2516-3

DK books are available at special discounts when
purchased in bulk for sales promotions, premiums,
fund-raising, or educational use. For details, contact:
DK Publishing Special Markets,
1450 Broadway, Suite 801, New York, NY 10018
SpecialSales@dk.com

Printed and bound in UAE

For the curious

www.dk.com

CONTENTS

HOW TO READ THE MAPS

A map is a drawing that gives an instant impression of a place. The maps in this book show India's states and union territories plotted with rivers, mountains, forests, and plains.

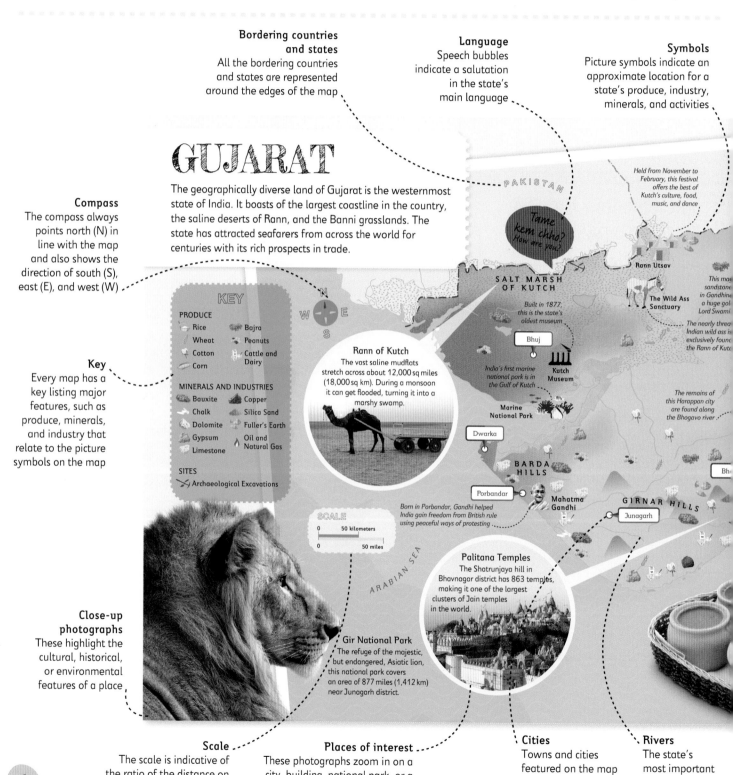

Bordering countries and states
All the bordering countries and states are represented around the edges of the map

Language
Speech bubbles indicate a salutation in the state's main language

Symbols
Picture symbols indicate an approximate location for a state's produce, industry, minerals, and activities

GUJARAT

The geographically diverse land of Gujarat is the westernmost state of India. It boasts of the largest coastline in the country, the saline deserts of Rann, and the Banni grasslands. The state has attracted seafarers from across the world for centuries with its rich prospects in trade.

Compass
The compass always points north (N) in line with the map and also shows the direction of south (S), east (E), and west (W)

Key
Every map has a key listing major features, such as produce, minerals, and industry that relate to the picture symbols on the map

KEY

PRODUCE
- Rice
- Wheat
- Cotton
- Corn
- Bajra
- Peanuts
- Cattle and Dairy

MINERALS AND INDUSTRIES
- Bauxite
- Chalk
- Dolomite
- Gypsum
- Limestone
- Copper
- Silica Sand
- Fuller's Earth
- Oil and Natural Gas

SITES
- Archaeological Excavations

PAKISTAN

Tame kem chho? How are you?

Held from November to February, this festival offers the best of Kutch's culture, food, music, and dance

SALT MARSH OF KUTCH

Rann Utsav

The Wild Ass Sanctuary

This ma... sandstone... in Gandhin... a huge gol... Lord Swami...

Built in 1877, this is the state's oldest museum

Bhuj

Kutch Museum

The nearly threa... Indian wild ass is... exclusively found... the Rann of Kute...

India's first marine national park is in the Gulf of Kutch

Marine National Park

The remains of this Harappan city are found along the Bhogavo river

Dwarka

BARDA HILLS

Bh...

Rann of Kutch
The vast saline mudflats stretch across about 12,000 sq miles (18,000 sq km). During a monsoon it can get flooded, turning it into a marshy swamp.

Porbandar

Mahatma Gandhi

GIRNAR HILLS

Junagarh

Born in Porbandar, Gandhi helped India gain freedom from British rule using peaceful ways of protesting

SCALE
0   50 kilometers
0   50 miles

ARABIAN SEA

Palitana Temples
The Shatrunjaya hill in Bhavnagar district has 863 temples, making it one of the largest clusters of Jain temples in the world.

Close-up photographs
These highlight the cultural, historical, or environmental features of a place

Gir National Park
The refuge of the majestic, but endangered, Asiatic lion, this national park covers an area of 877 miles (1,412 km) near Junagarh district.

Scale
The scale is indicative of the ratio of the distance on the map to the actual distance on the ground

Places of interest
These photographs zoom in on a city, building, national park, or a geographical feature, indicating its location on the map

Cities
Towns and cities featured on the map are marked with a blue outline

Rivers
The state's most important rivers are shown on each map

4

Borders

International borders
The borders between countries are marked with a thick dot-dash line.

Disputed borders
Some countries disagree about where the border between them should be. These are shown with a dashed line.

State borders
The borders between states are marked with a thinner dot-dash line.

Ceasefire line
The military controlled borders between two countries are marked by a dotted line.

Capital
A state's capital city is marked with a red outline

Textiles and weaving
Gujarat is known for its h craftsmanship, intricate ery, and vibrant colors in s and weavings. A prime is the patola sari, which ade in the Patan district.

Patola

m Temple
ainagar

Adalaj Stepwell
bad
This exquisitely carved 15th-century stepwell near Ahmedabad is five stories deep

Anand

Vadodara

Aav jo Come again

Narmada

Raichand Deepchand Library
One of West India's oldest libraries is in Bharuch and has a collection of more than 200,000 books

Topi

Surat

Garbha Deep

While performing the Garba dance, men and women form circles around a shrine, which includes an clay lantern called a Garbha Deep

Gujarati cuisine
Largely influenced by Vaishnavism and Jainism, traditional Gujarati food is primarily vegetarian. It is known for its delicate flavors and textures, and has both sweet and savory dishes.

Dhokla

Illustrations
Approximate locations of historic sites, wildlife reserves, natural wonders, and some cultural symbols are represented with icons

Page numbers
The color of the circle matches the region opener and tells you which region you are in

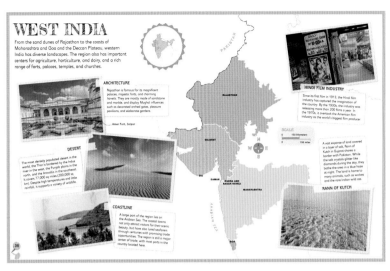

WEST INDIA

From the sand dunes of Rajasthan to the coasts of Maharashtra and Goa and the Deccan Plateau, western India has diverse landscapes. The region also has important centers for agriculture, horticulture, and dairy, and a rich range of forts, palaces, temples, and churches.

ARCHITECTURE
Rajasthan is famous for its magnificent palaces, majestic forts, and charming havelis. They are mostly made of sandstone and marble, and display Mughal influences such as decorated arched gates, pleasure pavilions, and elaborate gardens.

Amer Fort, Jaipur

DESERT
The most densely populated desert in the world, the Thar is bordered by the Indus river in the west, the Punjab plains in the north, and the Aravallis in the southeast. It covers 77,000 sq miles (200,000 sq km). Despite high temperatures and little rainfall, it supports a variety of wildlife.

COASTLINE
A large part of the region lies on the Arabian Sea. The coastal towns not only attract visitors for their scenic beauty, but have also lured seafarers through centuries with promising trade opportunities. The region is still a major center of trade, with most ports in the country located here.

HINDI FILM INDUSTRY
Since its first film in 1913, the Hindi film industry has captured the imagination of the country. By the 1930s, the industry was releasing more than 200 films a year. In the 1970s, it overtook the American film industry as the world's biggest film producer.

RANN OF KUTCH
A vast expanse of land covered in a layer of salt, Rann of Kutch in Gujarat shares a border with Pakistan. While the salt crystals glitter like diamonds during the day, they bathe the area in a blue haze at night. The land is home to many animals, such as wolves and the rare Indian wild ass.

Regional Maps

These maps show every state and union territory that is part of the region. Photographs highlight the features specific to the region.

Habitats

These colors depict the different landforms and natural vegetation of each state.

Snow-capped Mountains
High, rugged mountainous area, covered with snow. The subzero temperatures do not support much vegetation.

Alpine and subalpine
Mountains and high-elevation grasslands. Conifers are a common sight here.

Temperate
Region characterized by mild temperatures. The vegetation sheds leaves in winter. Grasslands are a common sight in this zone.

Dry Deciduous Forests
Areas where annual rainfall ranges 28–40 in. The vegetation sheds its leaves in summer.

Wet Deciduous Forests
This zone records an annual rainfall ranging from 40–80 in, and the vegetation sheds leaves in summer.

Tropical Evergreen Forests
This area receives very high rainfall, about 80–120 in annually. There is no fixed season for the vegetation to shed leaves.

Swamp or Littoral
Areas along the coast where the water table reaches right up to the surface.

Hot Desert
Dry and sandy areas, where only few thorny plants are able to grow.

ARCTIC OCEAN

NORTH AMERICA

North America
This huge continent lies entirely in the northern hemisphere of the world. It includes Greenland, which lies above the Arctic Circle.

PACIFIC OCEAN

ATLANTIC OCEAN

SOUTH AMERICA

South America
This continent lies mainly in the southern hemisphere and covers about one-eighth of Earth's land surface.

ATLANTIC OCEAN

INDIA AND THE WORLD

Antarctica
The world's southern-most continent, it is covered in ice and has the least population.

Europe
Though Europe is the second-smallest continent, it has the third-highest population.

ARCTIC OCEAN

ASIA

EUROPE

Asia
This is the largest continent in the world and has the highest population.

PACIFIC OCEAN

INDIA

AFRICA

India
The seventh-largest and the second-most populous country, India shares land borders with Afghanistan, Pakistan, China, Nepal, Bhutan, Bangladesh, and Myanmar.

INDIAN OCEAN

AUSTRALIA

Africa
It is the world's second-largest continent as well as the second-most populated one.

Australia
The world's smallest continent, it includes the world's biggest island, Australia, as well as New Zealand, and many small islands of the Pacific Ocean.

SCALE

0   2000 kilometers

0   2000 miles

SOUTHERN OCEAN

ANTARCTICA

THE INDIAN SUBCONTINENT

India is a distinct geographical entity with the Himalayan range forming its northern boundary, a peninsula bound by the Arabian Sea on its west, the Indian Ocean on its south, and the Bay of Bengal on its east.

The standard **meridian** of India is at 82.5°E longitude, passing through Mirzapur, Uttar Pradesh. This is the basis of the time observed throughout the country.

PHYSICAL MAP

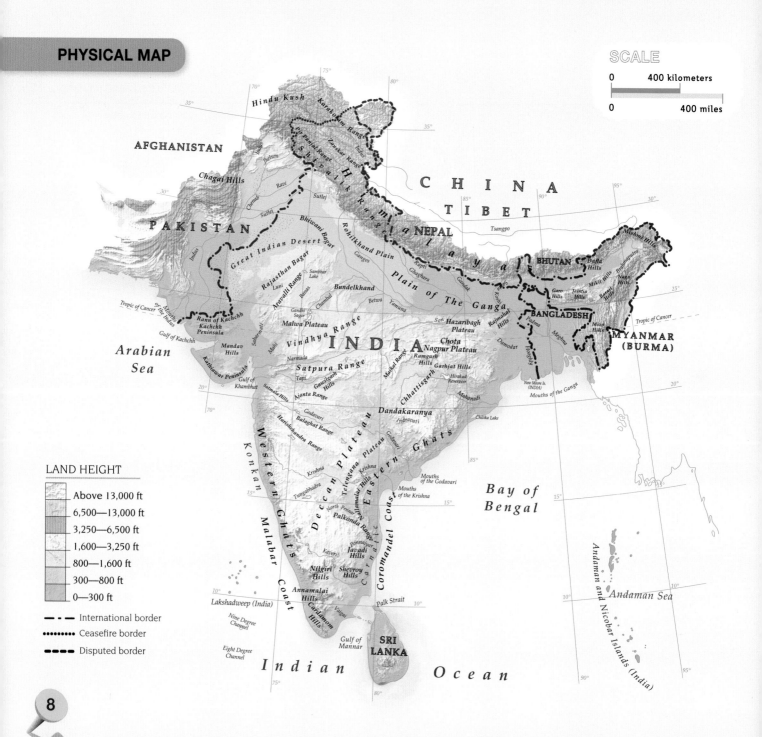

SCALE

0   400 kilometers

0   400 miles

LAND HEIGHT

Above 13,000 ft
6,500—13,000 ft
3,250—6,500 ft
1,600—3,250 ft
800—1,600 ft
300—800 ft
0—300 ft

– · – · International border
······· Ceasefire border
--- Disputed border

8

FACTS AND FIGURES

Capital New Delhi

Neighboring countries 8

Largest State (Area) Rajasthan

Smallest State (Area) Goa

Largest State (Population) Uttar Pradesh

Smallest State (Population) Sikkim

POLITICAL MAP

GEOGRAPHICAL HISTORY

The Indian subcontinent was once part of a supercontinent and used to be attached to Africa and Madagascar. In fact, all the continents in the world have changed shape over centuries and continue to do so. Here's how India and the rest of the world was formed.

PLATE TECTONICS
The Earth's crust is made up of huge, irregularly shaped pieces called tectonic plates. These plates move with the shift of hot molten rock, or magma, below the Earth's surface. This phenomenon is known as plate tectonics, and it leads to the movement of continents across the ocean bed. This is called continental drift. At the boundaries where the tectonic plates meet, three different types of movements can happen: divergent, transform, and convergent.

PANGEA
The present continents once formed a single land mass, the supercontinent Pangea. It existed about 300 million years ago.

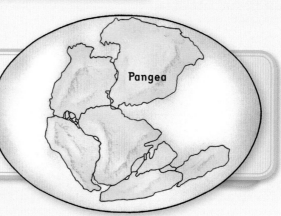

GONDWANA
About 200 million years ago, Pangea started splitting into two continents—Laurasia in the north and Gondwana in the south. Gondwana consisted of present-day India, Australia, Africa, South America, and Antarctica as one single land mass.

PRESENT LAND MASSES
The continents continued to move, and it is believed that India, Antarctica, and Madagascar separated from Africa around 180 million years ago. About 80 million years ago, India separated from Madagascar and drifted steadily northward, toward Asia.

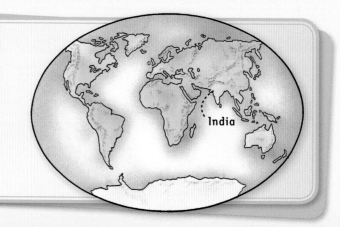

Plates moving apart

Plates moving past each other

Plates moving toward each other

Divergent movement
(Can lead to the formation of a new crust)

Transform movement
(Can cause earthquakes or tsunamis)

Convergent movement
(Can create volcanoes or mountains)

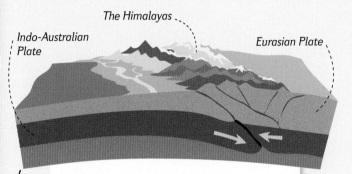

Indo-Australian Plate

The Himalayas

Eurasian Plate

RISING HIMALAYAS

As India continued its northward journey, it collided with the Eurasian Plate about 50 million years ago. This collision pushed up the sediments of the Tethys Sea to form the Himalayas and the Tibetan Plateau. The Indo-Australian Plate continues to push into the Eurasian plate, which is why the Himalayas continue to rise by around .4 in (1 cm) every year.

DID YOU KNOW?

The towering peaks of the Himalayas were once deep under the Tethys Sea, the water body that separated Laurasia and Gondwana. It is probably why marine fossils are commonly found on these mountains.

The Aravalli range

While the Himalayas are one of world's youngest mountains, the Aravalli range is thought to be one of the oldest geological features of the world. Once tall mountains, over time they have eroded down to hills and ridges.

The northern plains

The rivers flowing from the northern mountains filled the basin between Laurasia and Gondwana with deposits of sediments. This vast area, with its alluvial deposits, led to the formation of the fertile northern plains.

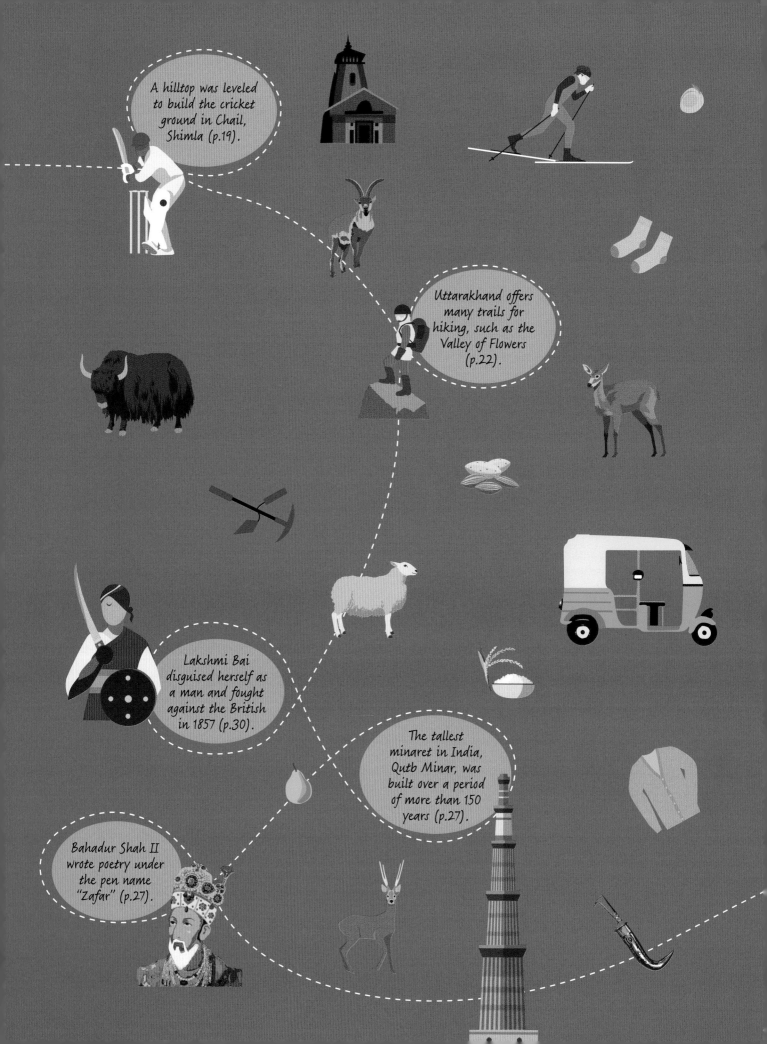

A hilltop was leveled to build the cricket ground in Chail, Shimla (p.19).

Uttarakhand offers many trails for hiking, such as the Valley of Flowers (p.22).

Lakshmi Bai disguised herself as a man and fought against the British in 1857 (p.30).

The tallest minaret in India, Qutb Minar, was built over a period of more than 150 years (p.27).

Bahadur Shah II wrote poetry under the pen name "Zafar" (p.27).

NORTH INDIA

Bound by the Himalayas in the north, with the river Ganga winding its way across the fertile plains, the northern region has six states. Delhi, the capital, is also here. It has been the seat of power for many empires, such as the Mauryas, Mughals, and British, who had a deep impact on the country's culture, literature, and architecture.

PAKISTAN

HIMALAYAS

The mighty Himalayas act as a natural barrier between Central Asia and the Indian subcontinent. Spread over 1,500 miles (2,500 km), it is among the world's youngest and highest ranges with 10 of its peaks towering above 26,000 ft (8,000 m). Subtropical jungles, temperate coniferous forests, and alpine meadows are in its vegetation zone. It includes many cultures and ecosystems.

SCALE

| 0 | 150 kilometers |
| 0 | 150 miles |

GANGES

Rising from the Himalayas, Ganges is one of the most important rivers in the country. Great civilizations have flourished on its banks through the ages. The river flows for about 1,600 miles (2,525 km), from the northwest to the southeast, through the mountains and vast plains that make up five Indian states, before draining into the Bay of Bengal.

MUGHAL ARCHITECTURE

Agra Fort

During their 300-year rule, the Mughals built many landmark monuments, including the Agra Fort and the Taj Mahal. The monuments are mostly made of fine marble and sandstone, and feature *charbagh* gardens, carved screens, and domes.

LADAKH

JAMMU AND KASHMIR

CHINA

HIMACHAL PRADESH

PUNJAB

UTTARAKHAND

HARYANA

NEPAL

DELHI

UTTAR PRADESH

N
W   E
S

CHAAT

Considered a north Indian invention, many popular forms of chaat trace their origin to the 12th century. This street food typically has a balance of sweet, sour, spicy, and tangy flavors.

FERTILE PLAINS

With rich deposits of alluvial soil, adequate water supply from the rivers, and suitable climate, the plains of north India are agriculturally rich. Punjab, Haryana, and Uttar Pradesh, with their lush green farms, are considered the breadbaskets of the country.

15

JAMMU AND KASHMIR

Known for its breathtaking natural beauty, lush gardens, and revered pilgrimage sites, Jammu and Kashmir is often referred to as "paradise on earth." The former state was designated a union territory in 2019.

KEY

PRODUCE
- Apple
- Saffron
- Silk
- Pear
- Walnut
- Sheep and Cattle

MINERALS
- Coal
- Gypsum
- Magnesite

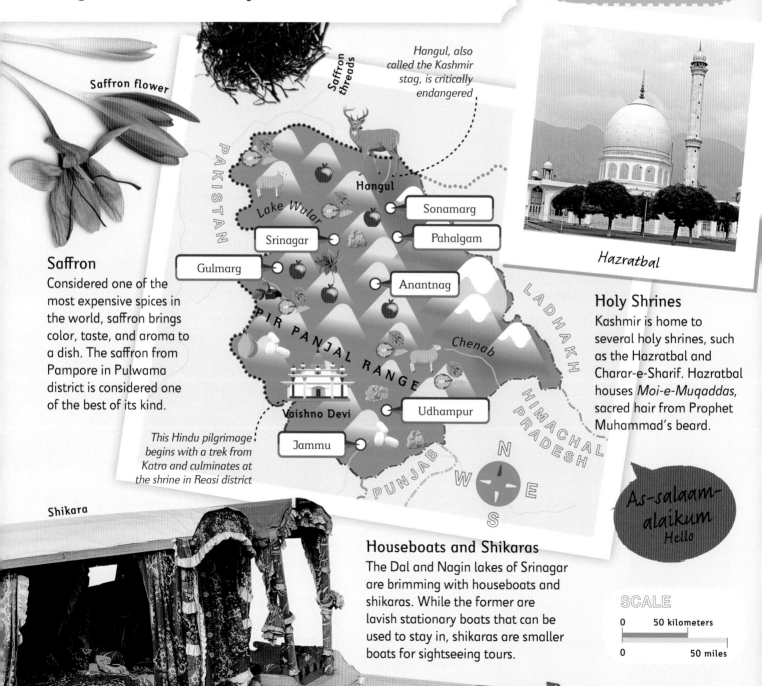

Saffron flower

Saffron threads

Hangul, also called the Kashmir stag, is critically endangered

Hangul

Sonamarg

Pahalgam

Srinagar

Lake Wular

Gulmarg

Anantnag

PIR PANJAL RANGE

Chenab

Vaishno Devi

Udhampur

This Hindu pilgrimage begins with a trek from Katra and culminates at the shrine in Reasi district

Jammu

PAKISTAN

LADAKH

HIMACHAL PRADESH

PUNJAB

N W E S

Saffron

Considered one of the most expensive spices in the world, saffron brings color, taste, and aroma to a dish. The saffron from Pampore in Pulwama district is considered one of the best of its kind.

Hazratbal

Holy Shrines

Kashmir is home to several holy shrines, such as the Hazratbal and Charar-e-Sharif. Hazratbal houses *Moi-e-Muqaddas*, sacred hair from Prophet Muhammad's beard.

As-salaam-alaikum
Hello

Shikara

Houseboats and Shikaras

The Dal and Nagin lakes of Srinagar are brimming with houseboats and shikaras. While the former are lavish stationary boats that can be used to stay in, shikaras are smaller boats for sightseeing tours.

SCALE

0 50 kilometers

0 50 miles

Lakes

Ladakh is known for its picturesque lakes, such as Pangong Tso and Tso Moriri. One of the country's highest lakes, Pangong Tso, does not support aquatic life, but acts as breeding ground for thousands of migratory birds every year.

Pashmina

Exquisitely embroidered, this soft and lightweight shawl is made from the hair of the Pashmina goat, found in the Changthang plateau in Ladakh.

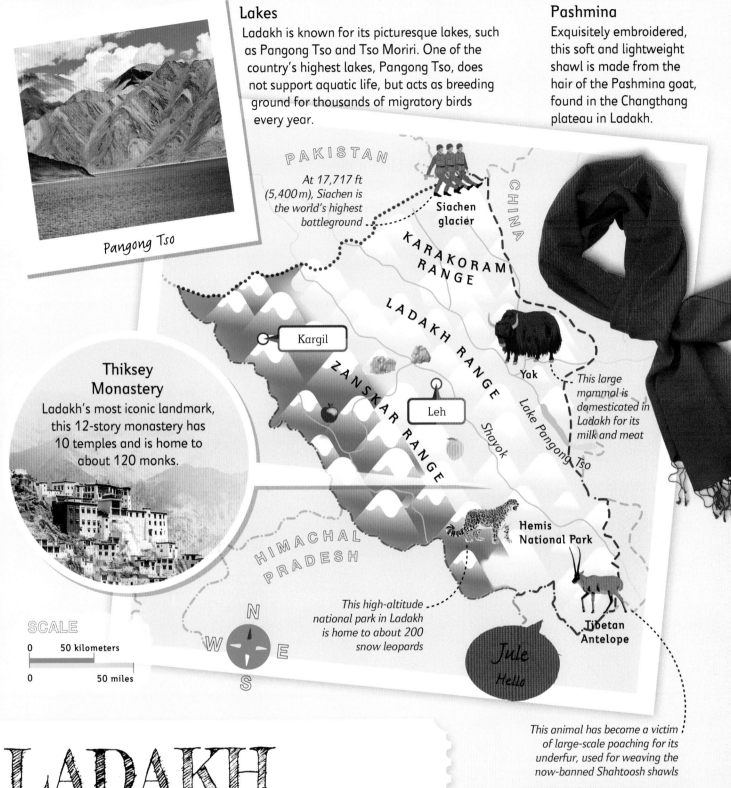

Pangong Tso

PAKISTAN

At 17,717 ft (5,400 m), Siachen is the world's highest battleground

Siachen glacier

CHINA

KARAKORAM RANGE

LADAKH RANGE

Kargil

ZANSKAR RANGE

Leh

Shayok

Lake Pangong Tso

Yak

This large mammal is domesticated in Ladakh for its milk and meat

Thiksey Monastery

Ladakh's most iconic landmark, this 12-story monastery has 10 temples and is home to about 120 monks.

HIMACHAL PRADESH

Hemis National Park

This high-altitude national park in Ladakh is home to about 200 snow leopards

Tibetan Antelope

Jule
Hello

SCALE

0   50 kilometers

0   50 miles

N W E S

This animal has become a victim of large-scale poaching for its underfur, used for weaving the now-banned Shahtoosh shawls

LADAKH

Carved from the former state of Jammu and Kashmir in 2019, the newly formed union territory of Ladakh is a sparsely populated, high-altitude desert with harsh climate. It is known for its mountain passes, pristine lakes, and Buddhist monasteries.

KEY

PRODUCE

🍎 Apple   Apricot

MINERALS

Gypsum   Magnesite

HIMACHAL PRADESH

This mountainous state gets its name from its geographical setting—*hima* means snow and *achal* means abode. With a rich variety of endemic flora and fauna; hill stations, popular and unexplored; and high lakes, gorges, and mountain passes, the state is a haven for nature lovers.

JAMMU AND KASHMIR

Folk musicians of the state play thonkru, *a traditional percussion instrument*

DHAULADHAR

Thonkru

Chamba

Dalhousie

This ornamental conifer is Himachal's state tree

Deodar Tree

Maharana Pratap Sagar

Rhododendron

This bright bloom is the state's official flower

KEY

PRODUCE
- Rice
- Corn
- Wheat
- Apples

MINERALS
- Barites
- Rock Salt
- Limestone
- Pyrite

ACTIVITIES
- Skiing
- Hiking
- Paragliding
- River Rafting

Snow leopard

Great Himalayan National Park
Located in the Kullu district, this national park was added to UNESCO's World Heritage List in 2014. It is home to a variety of animals, including the state animal, snow leopard.

Weaving
The state is known for its rich handicrafts, especially the weaving of lightweight Kullu shawls. These are famous for their bright colors and intricate geometric patterns.

Kullu shawl

Bhakra-Nangal Dam
Built on the Sutlej river in Bilaspur, this was India's first multipurpose river valley project and was inaugurated in 1963.

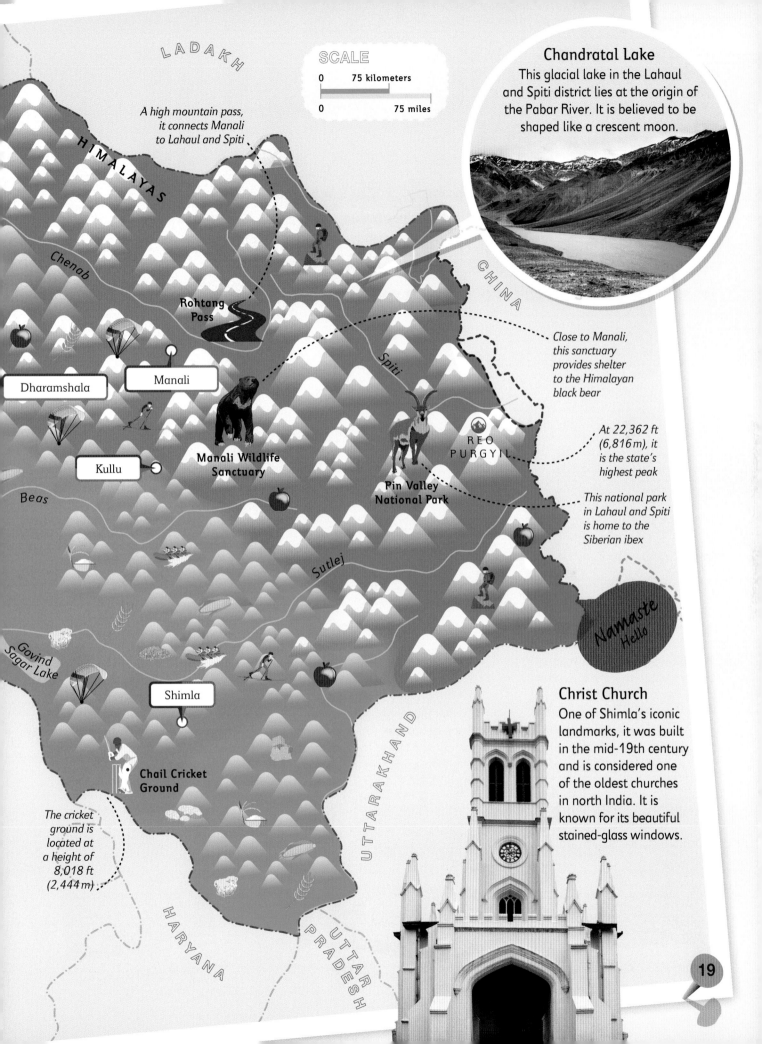

LADAKH

HIMALAYAS

SCALE

0   75 kilometers

0   75 miles

Chandratal Lake
This glacial lake in the Lahaul and Spiti district lies at the origin of the Pabar River. It is believed to be shaped like a crescent moon.

Chenab

A high mountain pass, it connects Manali to Lahaul and Spiti

Rohtang Pass

CHINA

Spiti

Dharamshala

Manali

Close to Manali, this sanctuary provides shelter to the Himalayan black bear

Manali Wildlife Sanctuary

Kullu

Beas

REO PURGYIL

At 22,362 ft (6,816 m), it is the state's highest peak

Pin Valley National Park

This national park in Lahaul and Spiti is home to the Siberian ibex

Sutlej

Namaste
Hello

Govind Sagar Lake

Shimla

Christ Church
One of Shimla's iconic landmarks, it was built in the mid-19th century and is considered one of the oldest churches in north India. It is known for its beautiful stained-glass windows.

Chail Cricket Ground

The cricket ground is located at a height of 8,018 ft (2,444 m)

UTTARAKHAND

HARYANA

UTTAR PRADESH

PHYSIOGRAPHIC DIVISIONS

The seventh-largest country in the world, India's vast landscape has a wide range of physical features. These can be divided into six physiographic regions, each with their own distinct characteristics, which impact the vegetation and the people inhabiting them.

THE HIMALAYAN MOUNTAINS

Stretching over the northern borders of India, these are some of the world's loftiest mountains. They consist of three parallel ranges—Greater Himalayas, Lesser Himalayas, and the Shivalik Hills.

THE NORTHERN PLAINS

The interplay of three major river systems—Indus, Ganga, and Brahmaputra—forms these expansive plains at the foothills of the Himalayas. The deposition of alluvial soil makes the plains fertile and favorable for agriculture.

THE PENINSULAR PLATEAU

A tableland of rocks formed due to the breaking of Gondwana (p.10), this plateau is among Earth's oldest land masses. It has broad, shallow valleys and rounded hills. It is primarily divided into the Deccan Plateau and the Central Highlands.

KEY CHARACTERISTICS OF THE PHYSIOGRAPHIC DIVISIONS

1 The higher ranges of the Himalayas are covered with summer grasslands or meadows, called *bugyals*.

2 The northern plains have fertile alluvial soil that supports a variety of crops such as wheat, rice, jute, and sugarcane.

3 A distinct feature of the peninsular plateau is the presence of black soil, which favors oilseeds, durra, tobacco, ragi, and corn.

4 The desert area is characterized by low vegetation cover that is mostly herbaceous, scrub type, and drought-resistant.

5 Malabar coast, the southern part of the western coast of India, has *kayals*, or backwaters, that are used extensively for fishing.

6 The island groups, Andaman and Nicobar and Lakshadweep, lie close to the equator, and so support dense tropical forests.

THE DESERT

The Thar Desert lies toward the western margins of the Aravalli Range. The vast region is covered with sand dunes. The arid area receives scanty rainfall and experiences the country's highest temperatures during the months of May and June.

THE COASTAL PLAINS

India has a long coastline running along the Bay of Bengal on the east and the Arabian Sea on the west. While the western coast stretches from Maharashtra to Kerala, the wider eastern coast extends from West Bengal to Tamil Nadu.

THE ISLANDS

There are two major island groups in India—the Andaman and Nicobar Islands (pp.114–15) in the Bay of Bengal and Lakshadweep (p.119) in the Arabian Sea. The former are volcanic islands and the latter are coral islands.

UTTARAKHAND

The mountainous areas of Uttar Pradesh were carved out to form Uttarakhand in the year 2000. The state shares borders with the Tibet Autonomous Region of China and Nepal. Peppered with Hindu religious sites, Uttarakhand is also called *Dev Bhoomi*, or the "Land of the Gods."

Corbett National Park
India's first national park, Corbett also marks the site of the launch of Project Tiger.

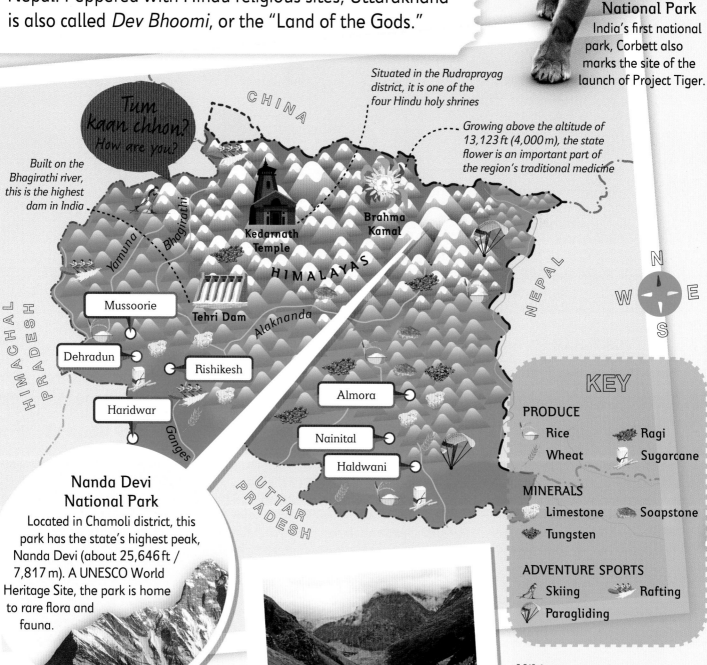

Situated in the Rudraprayag district, it is one of the four Hindu holy shrines

Tum kaan chhon? How are you?

Built on the Bhagirathi river, this is the highest dam in India

Growing above the altitude of 13,123 ft (4,000 m), the state flower is an important part of the region's traditional medicine

CHINA

Yamuna

Bhagirathi

Kedarnath Temple

Brahma Kamal

HIMALAYAS

Tehri Dam

Alaknanda

Mussoorie

Dehradun

Rishikesh

Ganges

Haridwar

Almora

Nainital

Haldwani

NEPAL

HIMACHAL PRADESH

UTTAR PRADESH

N
W — E
S

KEY

PRODUCE
- Rice
- Ragi
- Wheat
- Sugarcane

MINERALS
- Limestone
- Soapstone
- Tungsten

ADVENTURE SPORTS
- Skiing
- Rafting
- Paragliding

Nanda Devi National Park
Located in Chamoli district, this park has the state's highest peak, Nanda Devi (about 25,646 ft / 7,817 m). A UNESCO World Heritage Site, the park is home to rare flora and fauna.

Valley of Flowers

Hiking
The state is a popular hiking destination and has a range of trails to offer. Known for its endemic flowers, the Valley of Flowers National Park has some of the state's most beautiful hikes.

SCALE

0 — 50 kilometers

0 — 50 miles

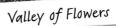

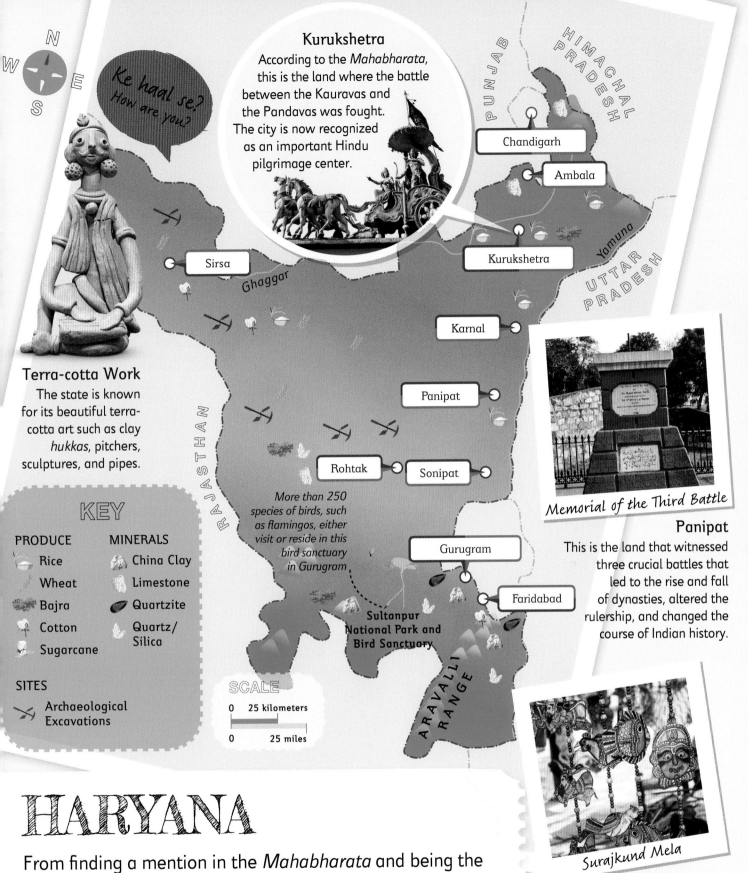

Ke haal se? How are you?

Kurukshetra
According to the *Mahabharata*, this is the land where the battle between the Kauravas and the Pandavas was fought. The city is now recognized as an important Hindu pilgrimage center.

PUNJAB

HIMACHAL PRADESH

Chandigarh

Ambala

Kurukshetra

Yamuna

UTTAR PRADESH

Sirsa

Ghaggar

Karnal

Panipat

Rohtak

Sonipat

RAJASTHAN

More than 250 species of birds, such as flamingos, either visit or reside in this bird sanctuary in Gurugram

Gurugram

Faridabad

Sultanpur National Park and Bird Sanctuary

ARAVALLI RANGE

Terra-cotta Work
The state is known for its beautiful terra-cotta art such as clay *hukkas*, pitchers, sculptures, and pipes.

KEY

PRODUCE
- Rice
- Wheat
- Bajra
- Cotton
- Sugarcane

MINERALS
- China Clay
- Limestone
- Quartzite
- Quartz/ Silica

SITES
- Archaeological Excavations

SCALE
| 0 | 25 kilometers |
| 0 | 25 miles |

Memorial of the Third Battle

Panipat
This is the land that witnessed three crucial battles that led to the rise and fall of dynasties, altered the rulership, and changed the course of Indian history.

Surajkund Mela

Crafts Festival
An annual congregation of Indian folk artists, this extravagant festival in Faridabad celebrates India's many colorful crafts, folk traditions, and delicious foods.

HARYANA

From finding a mention in the *Mahabharata* and being the site of numerous archaeological excavations to witnessing many incursions and being the battleground for pivotal wars, Haryana has immense historical significance. Situated in the Ganga plains, it is also an agriculturally prosperous state.

PUNJAB

This state is known for its vitality that shines through its energetic folk dances, hearty food, and spirited people. *Panj* means five and *aab* means water—a reference to the five rivers that used to flow through the state. The rivers and *doabs*, or tracts of fertile land, ensure very high agricultural yields for the farmers.

JAMMU AND KASHMIR

This mud fortress was built in the 1760s by Gujar Singh Bhangi, a local chieftain

Ravi

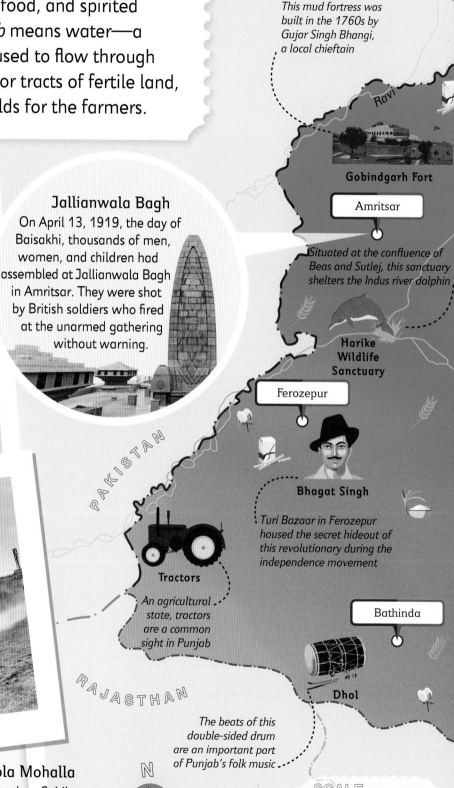

Gobindgarh Fort

Amritsar

Situated at the confluence of Beas and Sutlej, this sanctuary shelters the Indus river dolphin

Tussi kiven ho? How are you?

Jallianwala Bagh
On April 13, 1919, the day of Baisakhi, thousands of men, women, and children had assembled at Jallianwala Bagh in Amritsar. They were shot by British soldiers who fired at the unarmed gathering without warning.

Phulkari
Literally meaning "flower work," this style of embroidery is made with colorful silk threads. Used on special occasions such as weddings, phulkari was traditionally woven only by women.

Harike Wildlife Sanctuary

Ferozepur

Bhagat Singh

Turi Bazaar in Ferozepur housed the secret hideout of this revolutionary during the independence movement

PAKISTAN

Tractors

An agricultural state, tractors are a common sight in Punjab

Bathinda

Horseback riding

Hola Mohalla
Celebrated a day after Holi in Anandpur Sahib, this festival was instituted by Guru Gobind Singh for Sikhs to practice and display military skills, such as horseback riding and sword fights.

RAJASTHAN

Dhol

The beats of this double-sided drum are an important part of Punjab's folk music

N W E S

SCALE

0   25 kilometers

0   25 miles

24

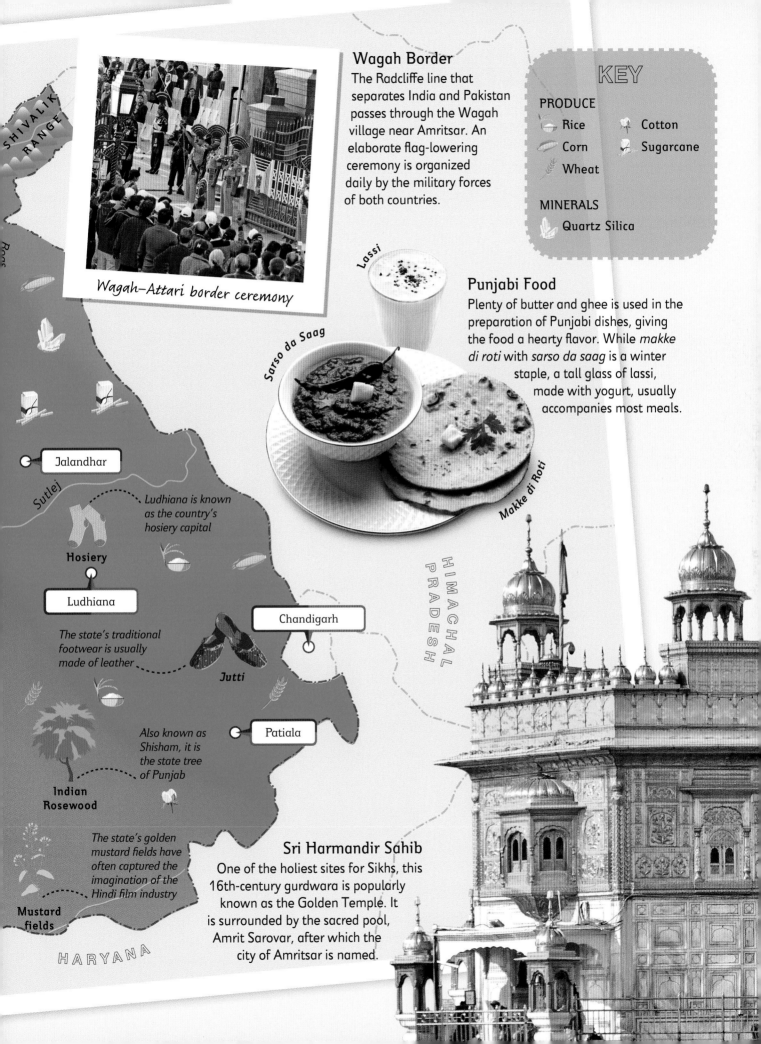

Wagah Border
The Radcliffe line that separates India and Pakistan passes through the Wagah village near Amritsar. An elaborate flag-lowering ceremony is organized daily by the military forces of both countries.

Wagah–Attari border ceremony

KEY
PRODUCE
- Rice
- Corn
- Wheat
- Cotton
- Sugarcane

MINERALS
- Quartz Silica

Lassi

Sarso da Saag

Punjabi Food
Plenty of butter and ghee is used in the preparation of Punjabi dishes, giving the food a hearty flavor. While *makke di roti* with *sarso da saag* is a winter staple, a tall glass of lassi, made with yogurt, usually accompanies most meals.

Makke di Roti

SHIVALIK RANGE

Ravi

Jalandhar

Sutlej

Ludhiana is known as the country's hosiery capital

Hosiery

Ludhiana

The state's traditional footwear is usually made of leather

Jutti

Chandigarh

HIMACHAL PRADESH

Also known as Shisham, it is the state tree of Punjab

Patiala

Indian Rosewood

The state's golden mustard fields have often captured the imagination of the Hindi film industry

Mustard fields

Sri Harmandir Sahib
One of the holiest sites for Sikhs, this 16th-century gurdwara is popularly known as the Golden Temple. It is surrounded by the sacred pool, Amrit Sarovar, after which the city of Amritsar is named.

HARYANA

CHANDIGARH

The shared capital of Punjab and Haryana and a union territory, Chandigarh is the first planned city of India. It was designed by the Swiss-French architect Le Corbusier and the planning began in the 1950s. The city symbolized a newly independent nation.

Open Hand Monument

Capitol Complex
A UNESCO World Heritage Site, the Capitol Complex is an architectural marvel and comprises the city's seat of power—the high court, the secretariat, the legislative assembly, and the Open Hand Monument.

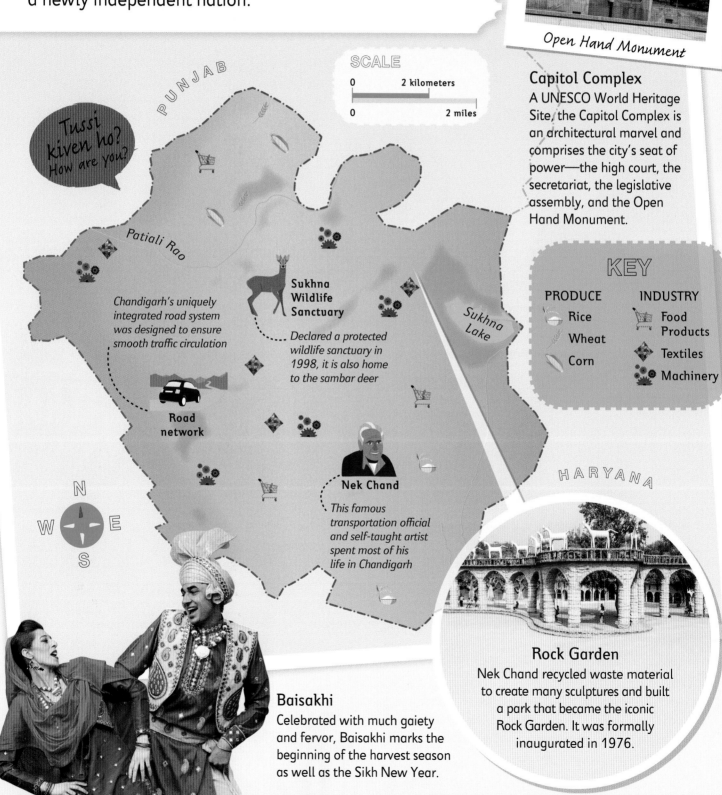

PUNJAB

Tussi kiven ho? How are you?

SCALE

0 — 2 kilometers

0 — 2 miles

Patiali Rao

Chandigarh's uniquely integrated road system was designed to ensure smooth traffic circulation

Road network

Sukhna Wildlife Sanctuary

Declared a protected wildlife sanctuary in 1998, it is also home to the sambar deer

Sukhna Lake

KEY

PRODUCE
- Rice
- Wheat
- Corn

INDUSTRY
- Food Products
- Textiles
- Machinery

Nek Chand

This famous transportation official and self-taught artist spent most of his life in Chandigarh

HARYANA

N W E S

Rock Garden
Nek Chand recycled waste material to create many sculptures and built a park that became the iconic Rock Garden. It was formally inaugurated in 1976.

Baisakhi
Celebrated with much gaiety and fervor, Baisakhi marks the beginning of the harvest season as well as the Sikh New Year.

DELHI

India's capital and a union territory, Delhi is situated on the fertile plains between the Yamuna river and the Aravalli hills. The second-most populous city, Delhi is also an eclectic mix of religions and cultures from across the country.

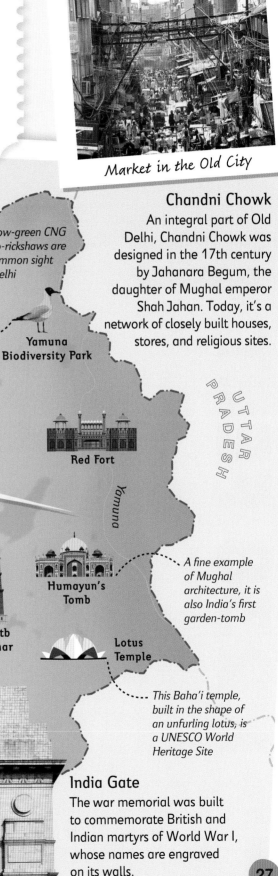

Market in the Old City

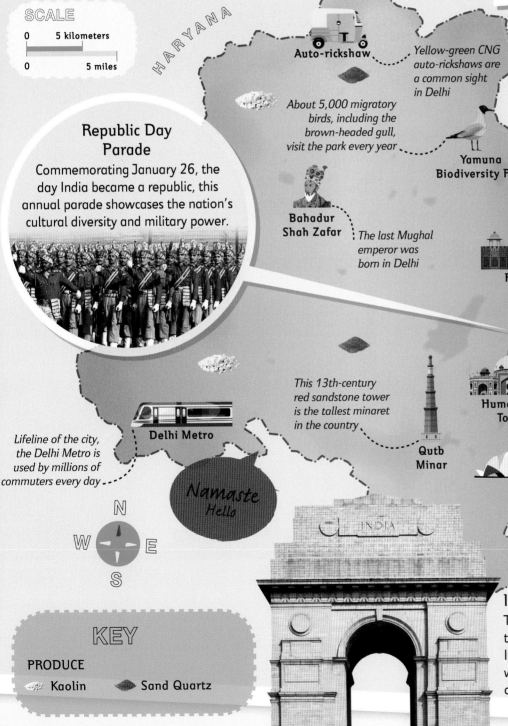

SCALE

0 — 5 kilometers

0 — 5 miles

HARYANA

Auto-rickshaw

Yellow-green CNG auto-rickshaws are a common sight in Delhi

About 5,000 migratory birds, including the brown-headed gull, visit the park every year

Yamuna Biodiversity Park

Chandni Chowk

An integral part of Old Delhi, Chandni Chowk was designed in the 17th century by Jahanara Begum, the daughter of Mughal emperor Shah Jahan. Today, it's a network of closely built houses, stores, and religious sites.

UTTAR PRADESH

Republic Day Parade

Commemorating January 26, the day India became a republic, this annual parade showcases the nation's cultural diversity and military power.

Bahadur Shah Zafar

The last Mughal emperor was born in Delhi

Red Fort

Yamuna

This 13th-century red sandstone tower is the tallest minaret in the country

Humayun's Tomb

A fine example of Mughal architecture, it is also India's first garden-tomb

Delhi Metro

Lifeline of the city, the Delhi Metro is used by millions of commuters every day

Qutb Minar

Lotus Temple

Namaste Hello

N W E S

This Baha'i temple, built in the shape of an unfurling lotus, is a UNESCO World Heritage Site

INDIA

India Gate

The war memorial was built to commemorate British and Indian martyrs of World War I, whose names are engraved on its walls.

KEY

PRODUCE

Kaolin   Sand Quartz

27

DELHI

India's capital has always been the seat of power for great rulers, embracing every empire's character. A melting pot of the old and the new, Delhi is studded with the remains of medieval empires, exquisite Mughal and Lutyens architecture, and sleek, contemporary buildings.

ORIGIN STORY

The capital city gets its name from Raja Dhilu, who founded the city and ruled in the 1st century BCE. It has since been known as Delhi, Dehli, Dilli, and Dhilli.

POPULAR CULTURE IN INDIA

The vibrant, mazelike, crowded lanes of Chandni Chowk have inspired many films, such as *Chandni Chowk, Band Baaja Baaraat, Delhi-6,* and *Black & White.*

POP

238 FEET

The height of Qutb Minar, India's tallest brick tower. This high, tapering monument has 379 steps that go all the way to the top.

WOW!

Red Fort was home to the Mughal rulers for almost 200 years. It was built during Shah Jahan's reign.

MAD ABOUT

Street food

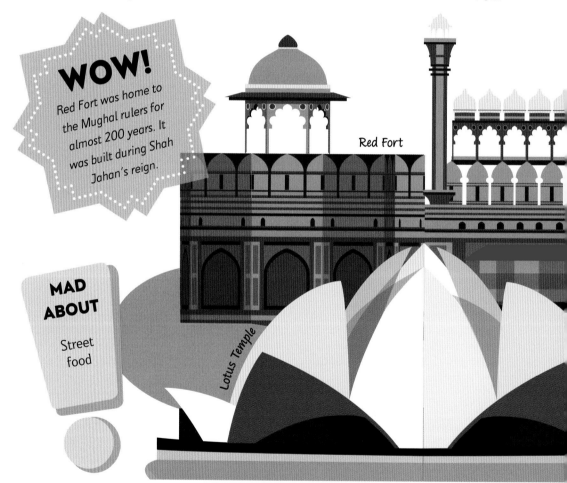

Red Fort

Lotus Temple

TOP 5

1 The **Rajpath** was designed during the British Raj. The area now has government offices and the residence of the President of India. It is the road through which the Republic Day parade passes every January.

2 Shaped as a giant white lotus, the **Lotus Temple** is a place of worship for the Baha'i faith. Its picturesque, green-landscaped gardens look even more beautiful in the evenings.

> "I asked my soul: What is Delhi?
> She replied: The world is the body and Delhi its life."
>
> Mirza Ghalib, poet

GREEN POCKET

Known as the lungs of Delhi, the hilly and forested Ridge is an extension of the Aravalli Hills. Cascading roots of the banyan, the medicinal neem, and the sweetly scented frangipani are just few of the many species found in the area.

PERSONALITY

From medieval poet and scholar Amir Khusrow to cricketer Virat Kohli, Delhi has been the birthplace of many famous people.

DID YOU KNOW?

Humayun's Tomb is one of the earliest masterpieces of Mughal architecture. Made of red sandstone and marble, it includes a Persian-styled *charbagh* and a pillared pavilion. This monument has been the inspiration behind the Taj Mahal and a muse to British architect Edwin Lutyens.

DELHI METRO

With more than 220 stations, the Delhi Metro is spread over the National Capital Region (NCR), encompassing Delhi, Gurugram, Noida, Faridabad, and Ghaziabad.

Qutb Minar

Delhi Metro

3 **Connaught Place,** the circular shopping district with white pillars, is in the heart of Delhi. It contains many famous cafes and restaurants.

4 The cultural hub at **Dilli Haat** is a popular crafts and gourmet bazaar, displaying the heritage of the country.

5 Artisanal parathas are popular in Chandni Chowk's narrow **Paranthe Wali Gali**. You can choose from a variety of fillings such as mint, beets, cheese, and chana dal.

UTTAR PRADESH

India's most populated state, Uttar Pradesh lies in the fertile Indo-Gangetic Plain. It has a number of landmarks, from the holy ghats of Varanasi to the Mughal monuments in Agra. The culturally vibrant land resonates with the beautiful dance movements of Kathak, stunning weaves of Banarasi silk, and mouthwatering Awadhi cuisine.

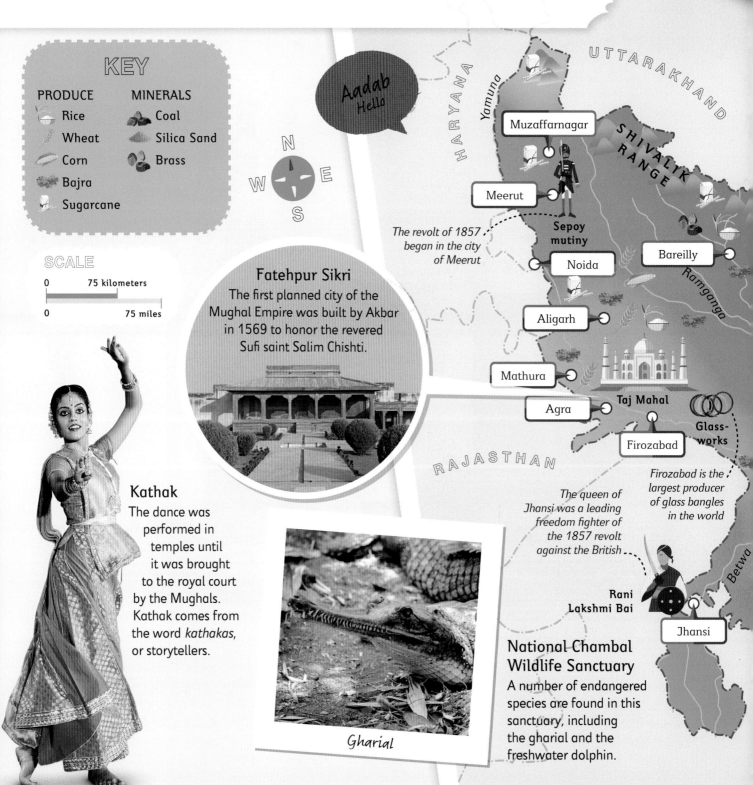

KEY

PRODUCE
- Rice
- Wheat
- Corn
- Bajra
- Sugarcane

MINERALS
- Coal
- Silica Sand
- Brass

Aadab
Hello

SCALE

0   75 kilometers

0   75 miles

Fatehpur Sikri
The first planned city of the Mughal Empire was built by Akbar in 1569 to honor the revered Sufi saint Salim Chishti.

Kathak
The dance was performed in temples until it was brought to the royal court by the Mughals. Kathak comes from the word *kathakas*, or storytellers.

Gharial

HARYANA

Yamuna

U T T A R A K H A N D

Muzaffarnagar

SHIVALIK RANGE

Meerut

The revolt of 1857 began in the city of Meerut

Sepoy mutiny

Noida

Bareilly

Ramganga

Aligarh

Mathura

Taj Mahal

Glass-works

Agra

Firozabad

Firozabad is the largest producer of glass bangles in the world

R A J A S T H A N

The queen of Jhansi was a leading freedom fighter of the 1857 revolt against the British

Betwa

Rani Lakshmi Bai

Jhansi

National Chambal Wildlife Sanctuary
A number of endangered species are found in this sanctuary, including the gharial and the freshwater dolphin.

Chikankari

This delicate hand embroidery from Lucknow is usually done on fine cotton. Traditionally, only white thread was used to make floral designs on the fabric.

Holi

This festival of colors is popular in the state and marks the coming of spring and the triumph of good over evil. People throw *gulal*, or colored powder at each other. This ritual is believed to be associated with Krishna throwing *gulal* at the *gopis*.

Holi at Barsana

NEPAL

More than 400 animal and bird species are found here, including the Bengal tiger

This park in Lakhimpur Kheri has some of the finest sal trees and is home to the swamp deer and the tiger

Pilibhit Tiger Reserve

Dudhwa National Park

BIHAR

Ghaghara

Lucknow

Gomati

Ayodhya

Gorakhpur

Ganges

GANGETIC PLAIN

Kanpur

Raebareli

Qawwali

These are devotional Sufi songs, usually performed live by a group of singers in an energetic style. The style uses percussion instruments, as well as clapping for rhythm.

Yamuna

Ashoka Tree

Prayagraj

Ganges

Varanasi

Ashoka, the state tree, has several medicinal properties

The Ganga and Yamuna rivers meet at Prayagraj

Kabir

JHARKHAND

The Ghats of Varanasi

Considered the holiest of Hindu cities, Varanasi has more than 85 ghats along the banks of Ganga, most of which are lined with temples. People go there to pray, bathe in Ganga's holy waters, and perform many rituals.

MADHYA PRADESH

Couplets, or dohas, by the 15th-century poet-saint Kabir, who was born in Varanasi, are still famous today

CHATTISGARH

SEASONS

The weather of a region is determined by its atmosphere over a period of time. Climate is the aggregate of weather conditions over a longer duration. India experiences four types of seasons, and falls in the "monsoon type climate," which means its climate is influenced by the monsoon winds.

 WETTEST PLACE

Mawsynram in Meghalaya is the wettest place in the world, with an average annual rainfall of 472 in (12,000 mm).

HOT WEATHER SEASON

▶ This season begins in March and goes through May–June.

▶ The temperature rises and varies depending on the latitude. Northern, northwestern, and central India experience high temperatures, ranging from 86°F to 113°F (30°C to 45°C).

Loo: A strong, hot, and dry wind that blows during the day and is a distinguishing feature of north and northwestern India during summer.

SOUTHWEST MONSOON

▶ Also called the approaching monsoon, this season begins in early June.

▶ Monsoon winds are forced to rise, cool, reach condensation levels, and shed moisture along the Western Ghats. This is why the Ghats get so much rain during the monsoons. In the north, monsoon winds enter from the northeast, and the northern mountains prevent them from leaving the country.

Rainfall in the Ganga valley decreases from east to west. Rajasthan and parts of Gujarat receive scant rainfall, and the northeastern states receive the maximum rainfall.

RETREATING MONSOON

▶ By October, the monsoon winds withdraw from the mainland and start moving back toward the Bay of Bengal.

▶ Also known as post monsoon, this season brings heavy rainfall in the southern states, mainly Tamil Nadu and Andhra Pradesh.

Due to high humidity and temperature, the weather in south India becomes very oppressive during this season.

COLD WEATHER SEASON

▶ The season ranges from mid-November to February in the northern states of India.

▶ The season is characterized by northeast monsoon winds that blow from land to sea.

▶ The peninsular region, however, does not have a defined winter season and the southern states do not show a change in temperature pattern.

The northeast trade winds lead to dry conditions in most parts of the country.

SOME FACTORS AFFECTING INDIA'S CLIMATE

LATITUDE

The Tropic of Cancer passes from the Rann of Kutch in Gujarat to Mizoram. The area on its south side has high temperatures throughout the year, while the area on its north experiences extreme temperatures.

RELIEF

High mountains, such as the Himalayas, act as barriers for moisture-laden winds from the seas causing rainfall. The mountains also prevent the extremely cold northern winds from entering the country.

THE DISTANCE FROM SEA

As the distance between the land and the sea increases, the moderating influence of the sea decreases. The climatic conditions of the areas closer to the sea remain almost the same throughout the year, but the areas far away show extreme temperatures.

ALTITUDE

As the altitude increases, the atmosphere becomes less dense and temperature decreases. With north India consisting of many high mountains and south India mostly being coastal plains, the temperature rises from north to south.

CLIMATE CHANGE

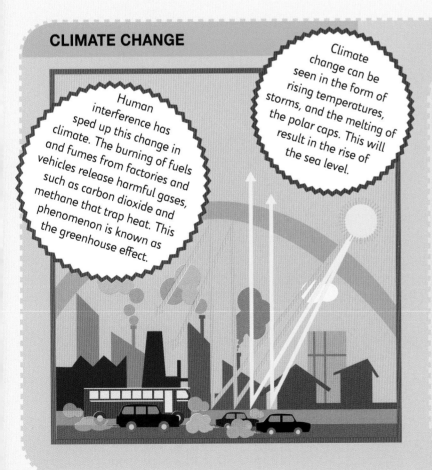

Human interference has sped up this change in climate. The burning of fuels and fumes from factories and vehicles release harmful gases, such as carbon dioxide and methane that trap heat. This phenomenon is known as the greenhouse effect.

Climate change can be seen in the form of rising temperatures, storms, and the melting of the polar caps. This will result in the rise of the sea level.

WHAT CAN WE DO?

1 Reduce the usage of resources that release greenhouse gases.

2 Walk, ride a bike, take a bus, or share vehicles.

3 Plant more trees—they absorb carbon dioxide and release oxygen.

Sand dunes keep changing in shape and size because of the pressure of wind. (p.38)

Did you know that the Indian bison is the world's largest bull? (p.51)

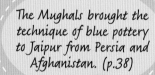

Rana Pratap Singh of Mewar and his warhorse Chetak have inspired many tales and poems. (p.39)

The Mughals brought the technique of blue pottery to Jaipur from Persia and Afghanistan. (p.38)

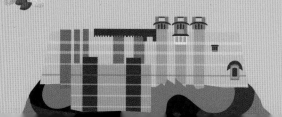

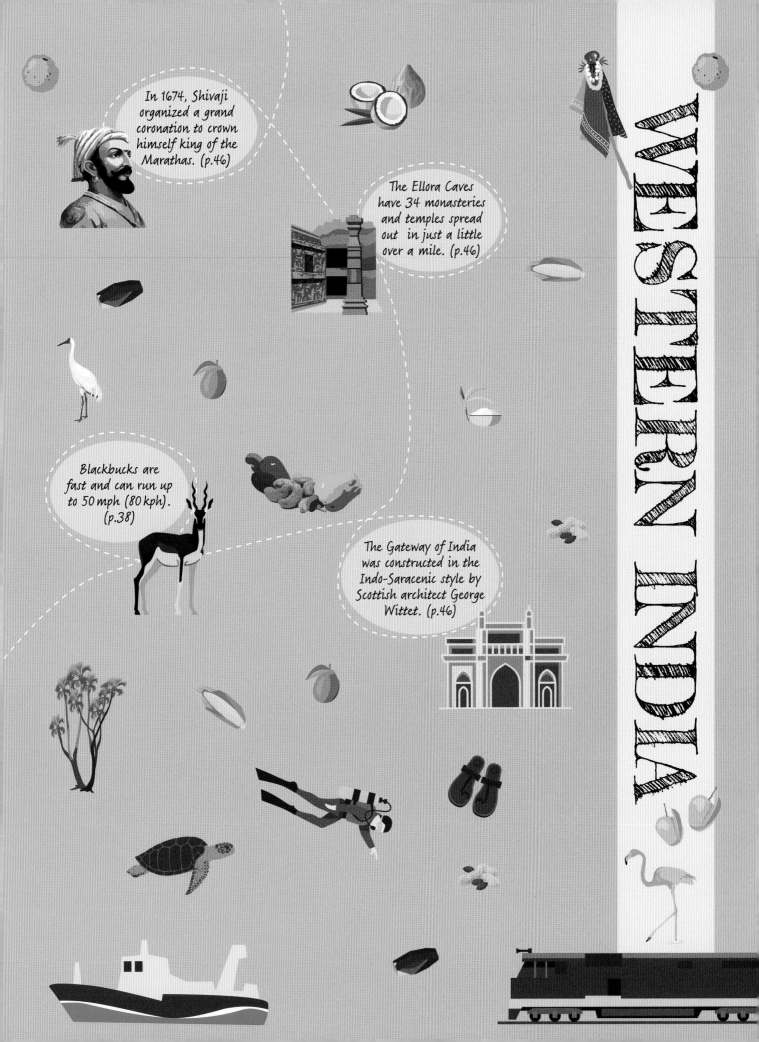

WEST INDIA

From the sand dunes of Rajasthan to the coasts of Maharashtra and Goa and the Deccan Plateau, western India has diverse landscapes. The region also has important centers for agriculture, horticulture, and dairy, and a rich range of forts, palaces, temples, and churches.

ARCHITECTURE

Rajasthan is famous for its magnificent palaces, majestic forts, and charming *havelis*. They are mostly made of sandstone and marble, and display Mughal influences such as decorated arched gates, pleasure pavilions, and elaborate gardens.

---- Amer Fort, Jaipur

DESERT

The most densely populated desert in the world, the Thar is bordered by the Indus river in the west, the Punjab plains in the north, and the Aravallis in the southeast. It covers 77,000 sq miles (200,000 sq km). Despite high temperatures and little rainfall, it supports a variety of wildlife.

COASTLINE

A large part of the region lies on the Arabian Sea. The coastal towns not only attract visitors for their scenic beauty, but have also lured seafarers through centuries with promising trade opportunities. The region is still a major center of trade, with most ports in the country located here.

HINDI FILM INDUSTRY

Since its first film in 1913, the Hindi film industry has captured the imagination of the country. By the 1930s, the industry was releasing more than 200 films a year. In the 1970s, it overtook the American film industry as the world's biggest film producer.

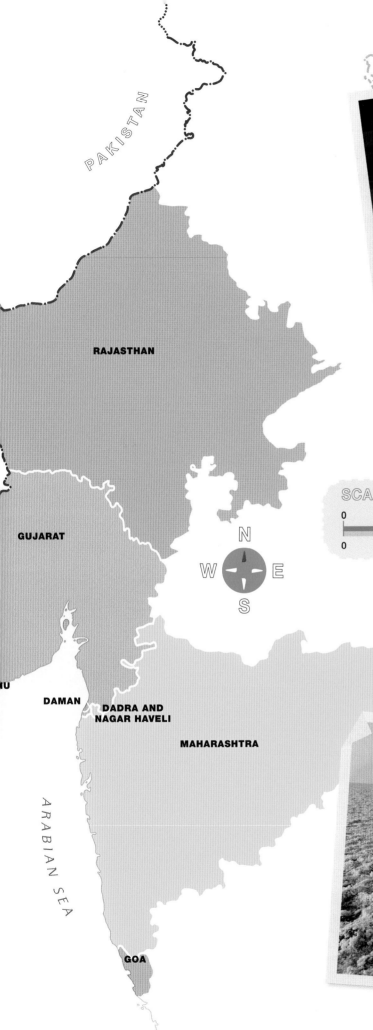

PAKISTAN

RAJASTHAN

GUJARAT

DAMAN

DADRA AND NAGAR HAVELI

MAHARASHTRA

ARABIAN SEA

GOA

SCALE

0 — 150 kilometers

0 — 150 miles

N W E S

A vast expanse of land covered in a layer of salt, Rann of Kutch in Gujarat shares a border with Pakistan. While the salt crystals glitter like diamonds during the day, they bathe the area in a blue haze at night. The land is home to many animals, such as wolves and the rare Indian wild ass.

RANN OF KUTCH

RAJASTHAN

Meaning "land of kings," Rajasthan is known for its majestic forts and palaces. Stretching more than 132,000 sq miles (342,000 sq km), it is India's largest state. The Aravallis divide it into two parts—the arid Thar Desert in the north-western region and the more humid and fertile southeastern part.

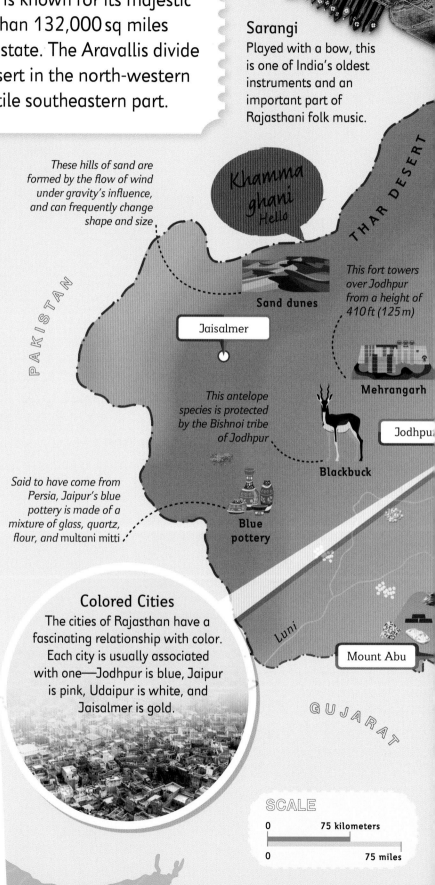

Sarangi
Played with a bow, this is one of India's oldest instruments and an important part of Rajasthani folk music.

KEY

PRODUCE
- Wheat
- Corn
- Mustard
- Durra
- Legumes
- Bajra

MINERALS
- Lead
- Asbestos
- Zinc
- Limestone
- Marble
- Calcite
- Copper
- Wollastonite

These hills of sand are formed by the flow of wind under gravity's influence, and can frequently change shape and size

Khamma ghani
Hello

THAR DESERT

Sand dunes

This fort towers over Jodhpur from a height of 410 ft (125 m)

Jaisalmer

Mehrangarh

PAKISTAN

This antelope species is protected by the Bishnoi tribe of Jodhpur

Jodhpur

Blackbuck

Said to have come from Persia, Jaipur's blue pottery is made of a mixture of glass, quartz, flour, and multani mitti

Blue pottery

Colored Cities
The cities of Rajasthan have a fascinating relationship with color. Each city is usually associated with one—Jodhpur is blue, Jaipur is pink, Udaipur is white, and Jaisalmer is gold.

Luni

Mount Abu

GUJARAT

Bandhani

Tie-dye Fabric
Fabrics are tied and dyed to create interesting designs in bright colors. The *bandhani* style uses dots, while the *lahariya* has a striped pattern.

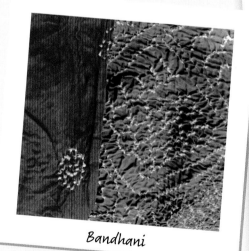

SCALE

0 ——— 75 kilometers

0 ——— 75 miles

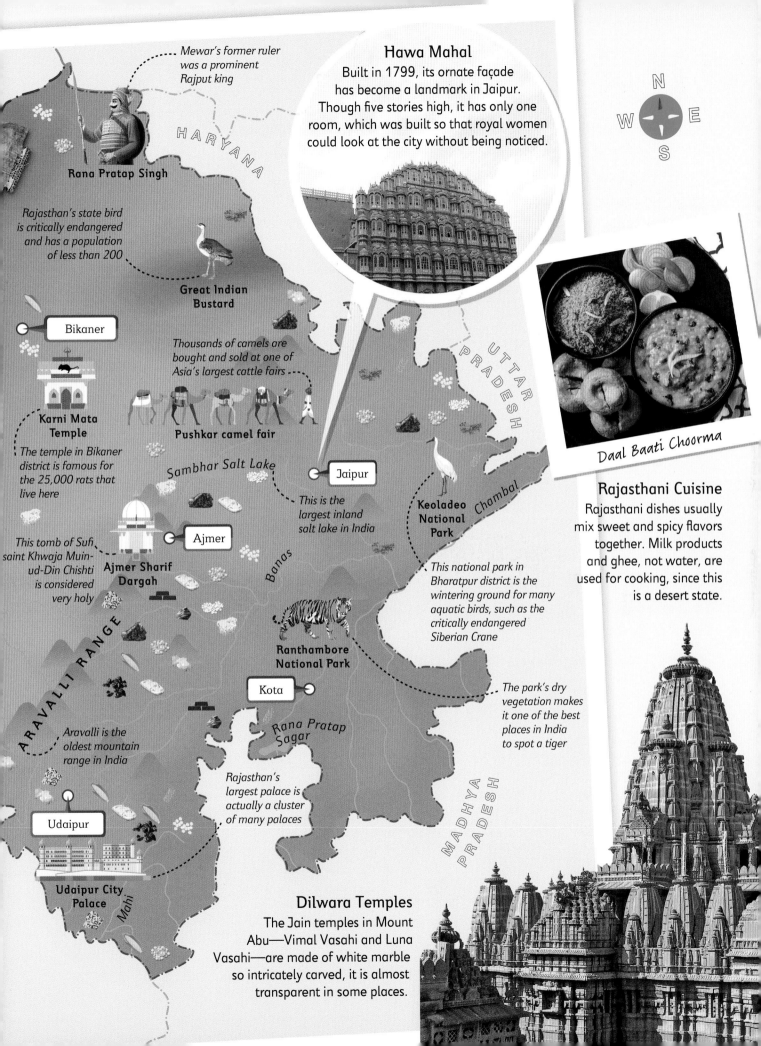

Mewar's former ruler was a prominent Rajput king

Rana Pratap Singh

HARYANA

Hawa Mahal
Built in 1799, its ornate façade has become a landmark in Jaipur. Though five stories high, it has only one room, which was built so that royal women could look at the city without being noticed.

Rajasthan's state bird is critically endangered and has a population of less than 200

Great Indian Bustard

UTTAR PRADESH

Daal Baati Choorma

Bikaner

Thousands of camels are bought and sold at one of Asia's largest cattle fairs

Karni Mata Temple

Pushkar camel fair

The temple in Bikaner district is famous for the 25,000 rats that live here

Sambhar Salt Lake

Jaipur

Keoladeo National Park

Chambal

Rajasthani Cuisine
Rajasthani dishes usually mix sweet and spicy flavors together. Milk products and ghee, not water, are used for cooking, since this is a desert state.

This is the largest inland salt lake in India

This tomb of Sufi saint Khwaja Muin-ud-Din Chishti is considered very holy

Ajmer

Ajmer Sharif Dargah

Banas

This national park in Bharatpur district is the wintering ground for many aquatic birds, such as the critically endangered Siberian Crane

ARAVALLI RANGE

Ranthambore National Park

Kota

Rana Pratap Sagar

The park's dry vegetation makes it one of the best places in India to spot a tiger

Aravalli is the oldest mountain range in India

Rajasthan's largest palace is actually a cluster of many palaces

MADHYA PRADESH

Udaipur

Udaipur City Palace

Mahi

Dilwara Temples
The Jain temples in Mount Abu—Vimal Vasahi and Luna Vasahi—are made of white marble so intricately carved, it is almost transparent in some places.

GUJARAT

The geographically diverse land of Gujarat is the westernmost state of India. It boasts of the largest coastline in the country, the saline deserts of Rann, and the Banni grasslands. The state has attracted seafarers from across the world for centuries with its rich prospects in trade.

PAKISTAN

Tame kem chho? How are you?

SALT MARSH OF KUTCH

KEY

PRODUCE
- Rice
- Wheat
- Cotton
- Corn
- Bajra
- Peanuts
- Cattle and Dairy

MINERALS AND INDUSTRIES
- Bauxite
- Chalk
- Dolomite
- Gypsum
- Limestone
- Copper
- Silica Sand
- Fuller's Earth
- Oil and Natural Gas

SITES
- Archaeological Excavations

Built in 1877, this is the state's oldest museum

Bhuj

Kutch Museum

India's first marine national park is in the Gulf of Kutch

Marine National Park

Rann of Kutch
The vast saline mudflats stretch across about 12,000 sq miles (18,000 sq km). During a monsoon it can get flooded, turning it into a marshy swamp.

Dwarka

BARDA HILLS

Porbandar

Born in Porbandar, Gandhi helped India gain freedom from British rule using peaceful ways of protesting

Mahatma Gandhi

SCALE

| 0 | 50 kilometers |
| 0 | 50 miles |

ARABIAN SEA

Palitana Temples
The Shatrunjaya hill in Bhavnagar district has 863 temples, making it one of the largest clusters of Jain temples in the world.

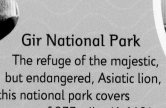

Gir National Park
The refuge of the majestic, but endangered, Asiatic lion, this national park covers an area of 877 miles (1,412 km) near Junagarh district.

Textiles and weaving
Gujarat is known for its rich craftsmanship, intricate embroidery, and vibrant colors in its textiles and weavings. A prime example is the patola sari, which is made in the Patan district.

Held from November to February, this festival offers the best of Kutch's culture, food, music, and dance

Patola

Rann Utsav

The Wild Ass Sanctuary

This magnificent sandstone temple in Gandhinagar has a huge gold idol of Lord Swaminarayan

The nearly threatened Indian wild ass is exclusively found in the Rann of Kutch

Akshardham Temple

R A J A S T H A N

Gandhinagar

Adalaj Stepwell

This exquisitely carved 15th-century stepwell near Ahmedabad is five stories deep

M A D H Y A   P R A D E S H

Ahmedabad

The remains of this Harappan city are found along the Bhogavo river

Lothal

Sabarmati

Mahi

Anand

Vadodara

Aav jo Come again

Narmada

M A H A R A S H T R A

Bhavnagar

G I R N A R   H I L L S

Junagarh

One of West India's oldest libraries is in Bharuch and has a collection of more than 200,000 books

Raichand Deepchand Library

Tapi

Surat

Chutney

Garbha Deep

While performing the Garba dance, men and women form circles around a shrine, which includes an clay lantern called a Garbha Deep

Dhokla

Gujarati cuisine
Largely influenced by Vaishnavism and Jainism, traditional Gujarati food is primarily vegetarian. It is known for its delicate flavors and textures, and has both sweet and savory dishes.

AHMEDABAD

The walled city of "Amdavad" has preserved its old-world charm and legacy in the face of rapid urban change. Its exquisitely carved monuments, traditional *pols*, gated streets, and mazelike bazaars stand proudly next to cutting-edge infrastructure and sleek modern buildings.

DID YOU KNOW?

Ahmedabad is the first Indian city to enter UNESCO's World Heritage Sites list, for being home to diverse, multicultural architectural structures. These include mosques and tombs, the finest Jain and Hindu temples, stepwells, bird feeders, and traditional *pols* that are home to huge families.

Amdavadi Pols

Indian Institute of Management

Makar Sankranti

IN HISTORY

On March 12, 1930, Mahatma Gandhi and 80 volunteers set out on a peaceful march from the outskirts of Ahmedabad to Dandi. It marked the beginning of the Salt Satyagraha. They walked about 240 miles (390 km) over 24 days to protest heavy taxation on salt. More than 50,000 people joined them along the way.

ADALAJ STEPWELL

This is one of the most elaborate stepwells, or *vavs*, in western India. It resembles a temple hall, with a labyrinth of pavilions, floors, balconies, and carvings of lotus motifs that cover the ornate walls.

Adalaj Stepwell

TOP 5

1 The final stage of India's freedom struggle began from the **Gandhi Ashram at Sabarmati.** In its vicinity is Gandhi's cottage, Hriday Kunj, which has been kept just as he had left it. His trademark round glasses are preserved here.

2 The **Jami Masjid,** which is made of yellow sandstone, was commissioned by Sultan Ahmed Shah and built in 1423. The mosque premises consists of 15 domes and 260 intricately carved pillars.

45

The number of stepwells in the Ahmedabad–Gandhinagar area. Built to acquire groundwater, they are engraved with Hindu, Jain, and Islamic motifs.

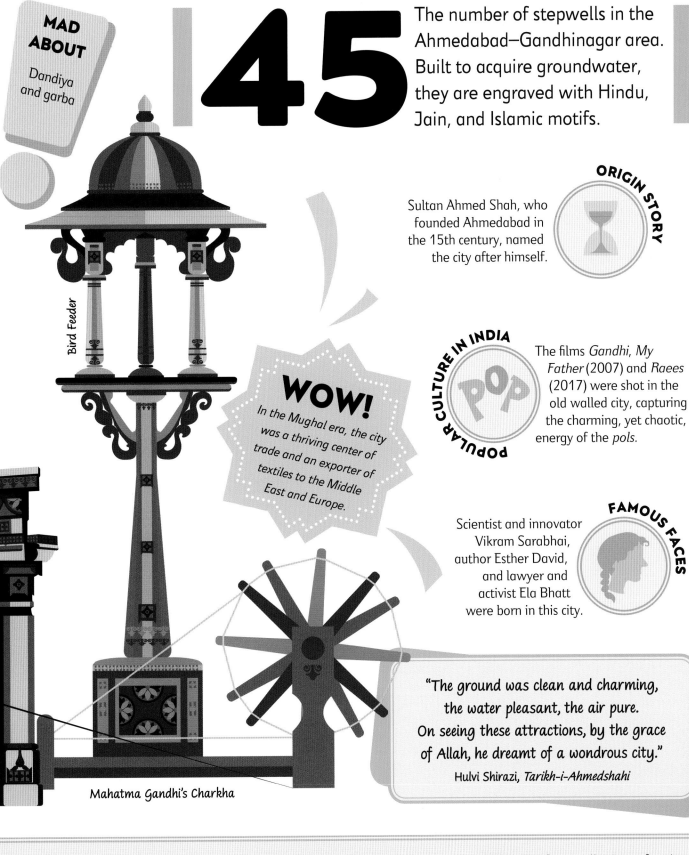

Bird Feeder

Mahatma Gandhi's Charkha

ORIGIN STORY

Sultan Ahmed Shah, who founded Ahmedabad in the 15th century, named the city after himself.

POPULAR CULTURE IN INDIA

POP

The films *Gandhi, My Father* (2007) and *Raees* (2017) were shot in the old walled city, capturing the charming, yet chaotic, energy of the *pols*.

WOW!

In the Mughal era, the city was a thriving center of trade and an exporter of textiles to the Middle East and Europe.

FAMOUS FACES

Scientist and innovator Vikram Sarabhai, author Esther David, and lawyer and activist Ela Bhatt were born in this city.

"The ground was clean and charming, the water pleasant, the air pure. On seeing these attractions, by the grace of Allah, he dreamt of a wondrous city."
Hulvi Shirazi, *Tarikh-i-Ahmedshahi*

3 From the **Bhadra Fort** there is a panoramic view of converging streets. In the 15th century, royal processions and polo games took place within its formidable structure.

4 The **Sidi Saiyyed Mosque's** famous and intricately carved "tree of life" latticework was carved in the 16th century.

5 The finest collections of antique and modern Indian textiles are showcased at the **Calico Museum of Textiles.** Some of them date back 500 years.

DAMAN AND DIU

The area is made up of two separate geographical entities. While Daman is a coastal town in south Gujarat, Diu is an island near the Junagarh district of the state. Both were merged with Dadra and Nagar Haveli in 2019 to form a single union territory.

Diu Fort
Built in the 16th century, when the Portuguese took control of the island, the Diu Fort is a landmark monument known for its double moat and old cannons.

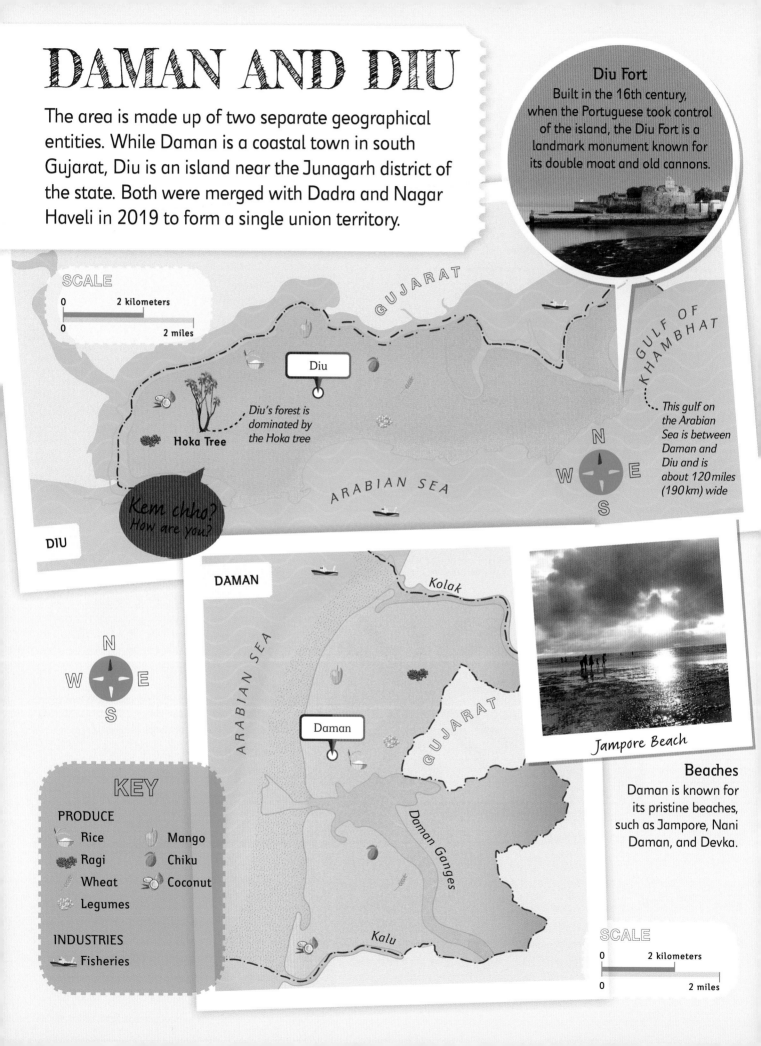

DIU

SCALE
0   2 kilometers
0   2 miles

GUJARAT

Diu

Diu's forest is dominated by the Hoka tree

Hoka Tree

GULF OF KHAMBHAT

This gulf on the Arabian Sea is between Daman and Diu and is about 120 miles (190 km) wide

ARABIAN SEA

N W E S

Kem chho?
How are you?

DAMAN

N W E S

Kolak

ARABIAN SEA

Daman

GUJARAT

Daman Ganges

Kalu

Jampore Beach

Beaches
Daman is known for its pristine beaches, such as Jampore, Nani Daman, and Devka.

KEY

PRODUCE

- Rice
- Ragi
- Wheat
- Legumes
- Mango
- Chiku
- Coconut

INDUSTRIES

- Fisheries

SCALE
0   2 kilometers
0   2 miles

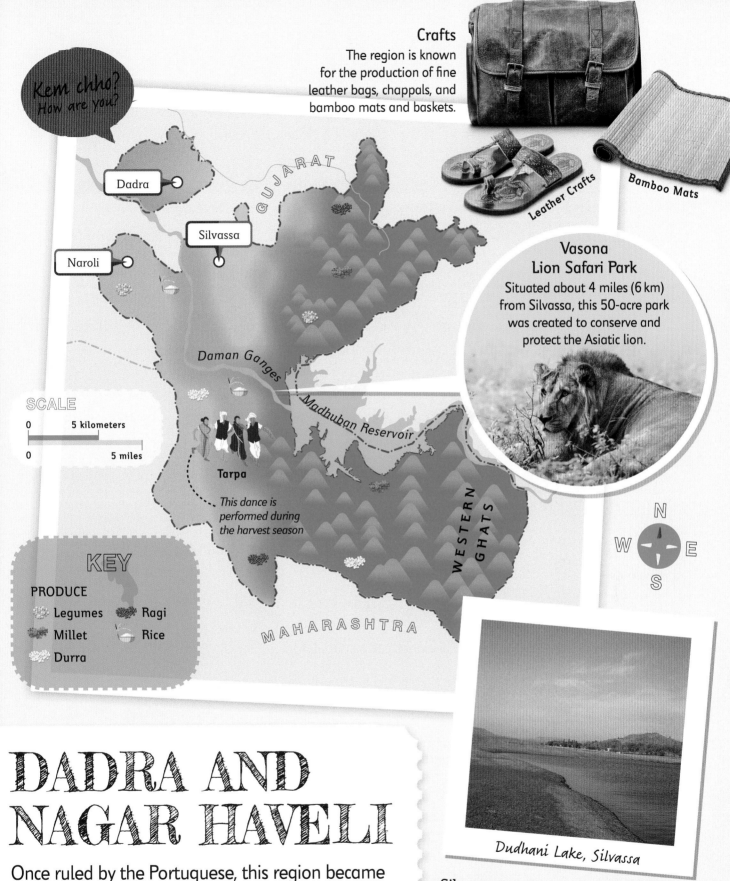

Kem chho?
How are you?

Crafts
The region is known for the production of fine leather bags, chappals, and bamboo mats and baskets.

Leather Crafts

Bamboo Mats

Dadra

GUJARAT

Silvassa

Naroli

Vasona Lion Safari Park
Situated about 4 miles (6 km) from Silvassa, this 50-acre park was created to conserve and protect the Asiatic lion.

Daman Ganges

Madhuban Reservoir

SCALE

0   5 kilometers

0   5 miles

Tarpa

This dance is performed during the harvest season

W E S T E R N   G H A T S

KEY
PRODUCE
- Legumes
- Ragi
- Millet
- Rice
- Durra

MAHARASHTRA

N
W   E
S

Dudhani Lake, Silvassa

DADRA AND NAGAR HAVELI

Once ruled by the Portuguese, this region became a part of the Indian Union in 1961 and a part of a single union territory in 2019. Nagar Haveli is wedged between Gujarat and Maharashtra. Dadra is an enclave surrounded by Gujarat on all sides.

Silvassa
During the Portuguese rule, Silvassa was known as Vila de Paco d'Arcos. Previously the administrative capital of Dadra and Nagar Haveli, Silvassa is an important economic center of the union territory.

45

MAHARASHTRA

Green hills and scenic coastal plains make up the state's varied landscape. The hills of the Western Ghats, source of many rivers, run parallel to the narrow Konkan Coast, while cradled in the center is the Deccan Plateau, formed from black volcanic lava. The state also has busy industrial, financial, and academic centers, and produces some of the country's finest fruits.

Modak

Solkadhi

KEY

PRODUCE

- Rice
- Corn
- Durra
- Legumes
- Cotton
- Sugarcane
- Peanuts
- Soybeans
- Mango
- Orange
- Chiku

MINERALS AND INDUSTRIES

- Bauxite
- Manganese
- Corrundum
- Hematite
- Oil and Natural Gas
- Fisheries

SITES

- Tiger Reserves

Namaskar
Hello

N W E S

GUJARAT

SATPURA RANGE

AJANTA

Nashik

Ellora caves

Aurangaba

The first train of the Indian subcontinent ran from Mumbai to Thane in 1853

These 34 caves in Aurangabad extend for more than a mile (2 km) on a basalt cliff

ARABIAN SEA

Railroads

Bhima

Mumbai

Shivaji

Born in Pune, he founded the Maratha Empire in the 17th century

Pune

This landmark was the first sight to greet sailors coming to India during the British Raj

Gateway of India

WESTERN GHATS

DECCAN PLATEAU

These sturdy, flat, handmade leather sandals have become famous across the country

Krishna

Ratnagiri

Kolhapuri sandals

Kolhapur

KARNATAKA

GOA

Elephanta caves

Dedicated to Lord Shiva, these 6th-century cave temples are located on Elephanta Island, 6 miles (10 km) off Mumbai's eastern shore.

Marathi cuisine

Marathi food often includes Konkani, Malvani, and Varadi cuisines. Konkani cuisine is spicy, Malvani cuisine is predominantly meat-based and uses coconut milk, and Varadi dishes often have peanuts and cashew nuts.

Thalipeeth

Gold Zari Weave in Paithani

Weaving

The fine art of the Paithani silk and zari saris goes back more than 2,000 years; the design is inspired by the flora and fauna of Paithan, a town in Aurangabad district.

This spring festival marks the beginning of the Marathi new year

MADHYA PRADESH

CHATTISGARH

GAWLIGARH HILLS

Nagpur

Gudi Padwa

SATMALA HILLS

Purna

Penganga

ANGE

Lavani

Performed exclusively by women, the subject of this song-and-dance form draws inspiration from the classics and present-day social issues

TELANGANA

Godavari

Nanded

Ajanta caves

A UNESCO World Heritage Site, the 30 caves at Ajanta date back to the 1st and 2nd century BCE and have paintings and sculptures that are considered masterpieces of Buddhist art.

Janmasthami Dahi Handi

SCALE

| 0 | 75 kilometers |
| 0 | 75 miles |

Haji Ali Dargah

This highly revered mosque and tomb is located on an islet, or a small island, in the Arabian Sea near Mumbai and can be approached by a long highway.

Popular festivals

A variety of festivals are celebrated in Maharashtra with great energy and joy. Ganesh Chaturthi, Janmasthami, and Holi are a few examples.

MUMBAI

Lined with coconut trees and narrow beach promenades and speckled with concrete high-rise buildings, black and yellow taxis, and energetic film sets, this is a city that never sleeps. Mumbai is the city that draws people in search of fame and fortune.

ORIGIN STORY

Captured by the Portuguese in 1534, the then-seven islands of Bombay were gifted to the British crown in 1661 as part of the royal dowry.

8 MILLION

The number of people who commute on the Mumbai local on a weekday, which is almost equal to the population of Israel!

WOW!
The first passenger train in India ran from Bori Bunder railroad station in Mumbai to Thane on April 16, 1853.

Chhatrapati Shivaji Terminus

SEA LINK

Connecting Bandra in the west of Mumbai to Worli in the south, the Bandra–Worli Sea Link is a 3.5 mile- (5.6 km-) long architectural marvel. It is India's first cable-stayed bridge built on the open sea. It has helped shorten travel time for many Mumbaikars.

TOP 5

1 Admire the **Chhatrapati Shivaji Terminus,** which is a blend of traditional Indian, Victorian, and Gothic Revival architecture. Designed by the British architect F.W. Stevens, this building is truly unique.

2 Located on an island close to Mumbai on the Sea of Oman, the **Elephanta Island,** is called the City of Caves. This popular landmark is known for its collection of rock art devoted to the god Shiva.

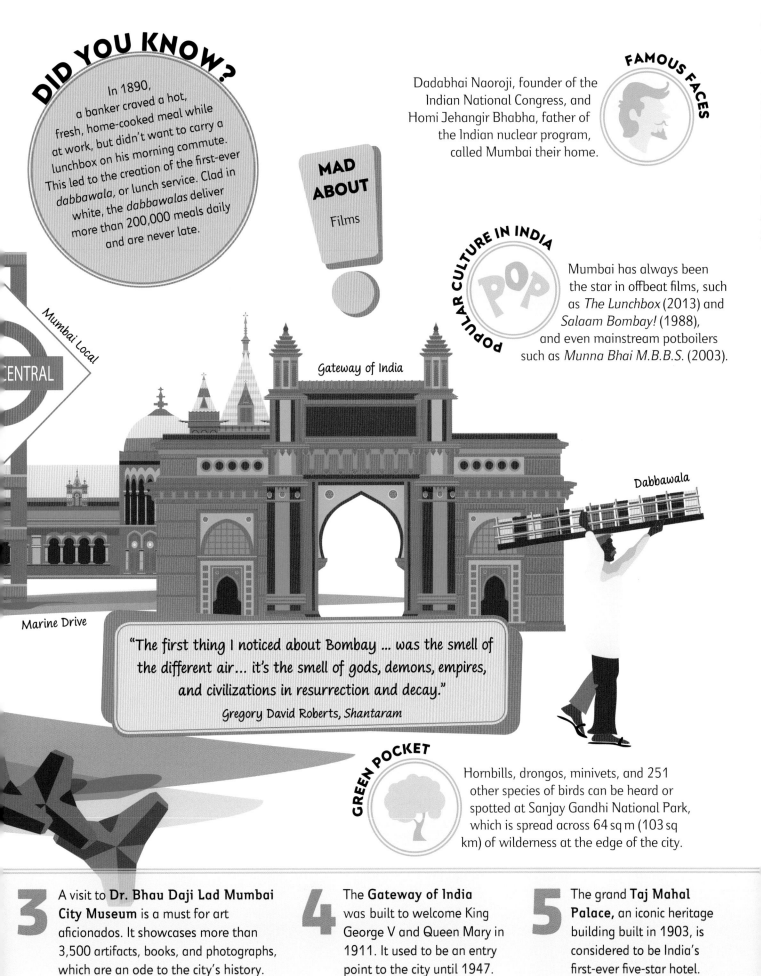

DID YOU KNOW?

In 1890, a banker craved a hot, fresh, home-cooked meal while at work, but didn't want to carry a lunchbox on his morning commute. This led to the creation of the first-ever *dabbawala*, or lunch service. Clad in white, the *dabbawalas* deliver more than 200,000 meals daily and are never late.

MAD ABOUT

Films

FAMOUS FACES

Dadabhai Naoroji, founder of the Indian National Congress, and Homi Jehangir Bhabha, father of the Indian nuclear program, called Mumbai their home.

POPULAR CULTURE IN INDIA

POP

Mumbai has always been the star in offbeat films, such as *The Lunchbox* (2013) and *Salaam Bombay!* (1988), and even mainstream potboilers such as *Munna Bhai M.B.B.S.* (2003).

Mumbai Local

CENTRAL

Gateway of India

Dabbawala

Marine Drive

"The first thing I noticed about Bombay ... was the smell of the different air... it's the smell of gods, demons, empires, and civilizations in resurrection and decay."

Gregory David Roberts, *Shantaram*

GREEN POCKET

Hornbills, drongos, minivets, and 251 other species of birds can be heard or spotted at Sanjay Gandhi National Park, which is spread across 64 sq m (103 sq km) of wilderness at the edge of the city.

3 A visit to **Dr. Bhau Daji Lad Mumbai City Museum** is a must for art aficionados. It showcases more than 3,500 artifacts, books, and photographs, which are an ode to the city's history.

4 The **Gateway of India** was built to welcome King George V and Queen Mary in 1911. It used to be an entry point to the city until 1947.

5 The grand **Taj Mahal Palace,** an iconic heritage building built in 1903, is considered to be India's first-ever five-star hotel.

GOA

On the Konkan coast, Goa, the smallest state in India, is a popular tourist destination. Its beautiful beaches give way to the green hills of the Western Ghats as you move toward the eastern part of the state. The 400 years of Portuguese rule have influenced Goa's culture and its people and the impact can also be seen in the state's architecture.

Goan cuisine

Considered incomplete without seafood and spices, Goan food is influenced by Portuguese flavors. The famous shrimp curry is cooked in coconut milk and has a spicy and sour sauce.

Goan shrimp curry

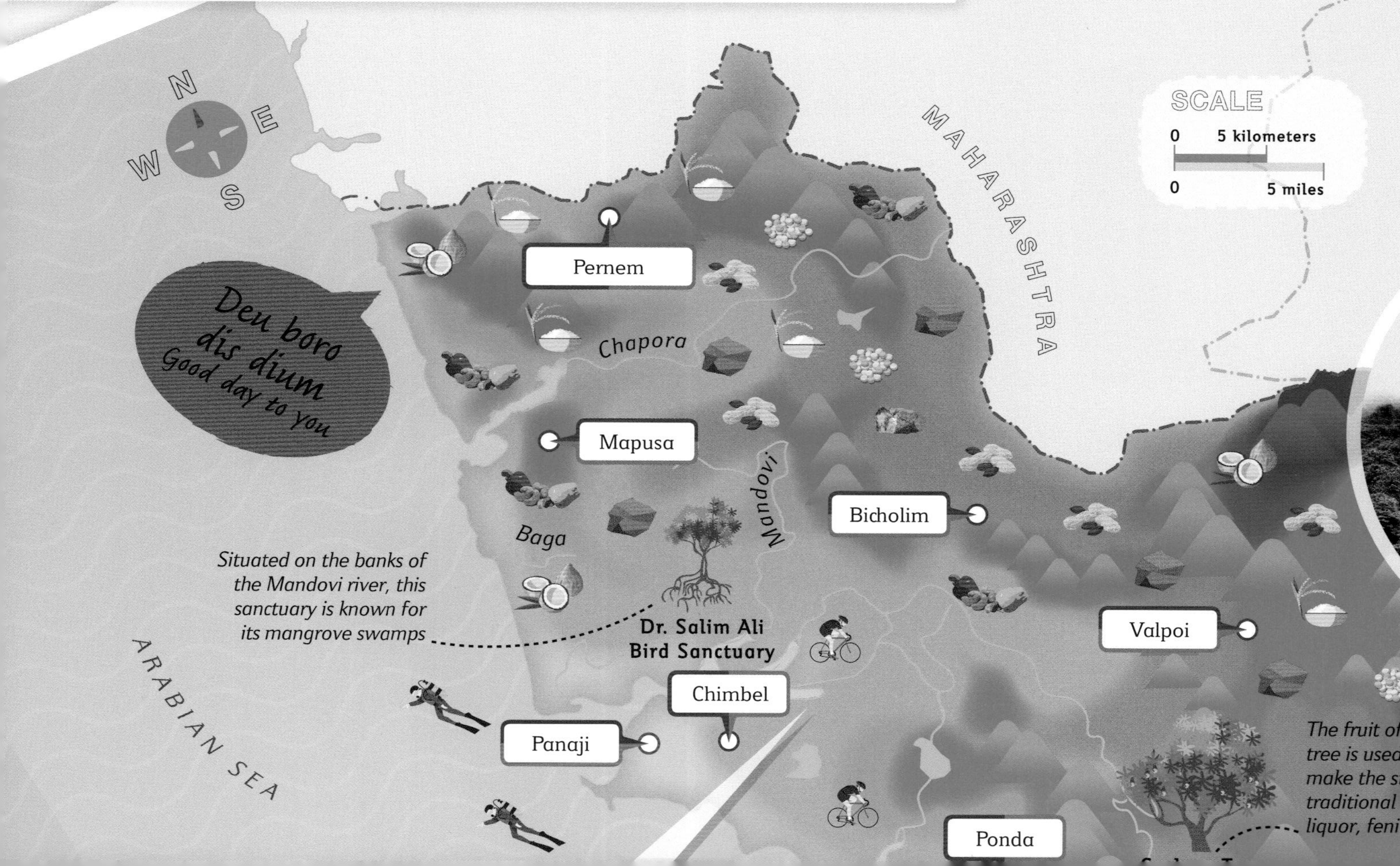

Dudhsagar Falls

Literally meaning a "sea of milk," the waterfall on Mandovi river is known for the white spray and foam it creates.

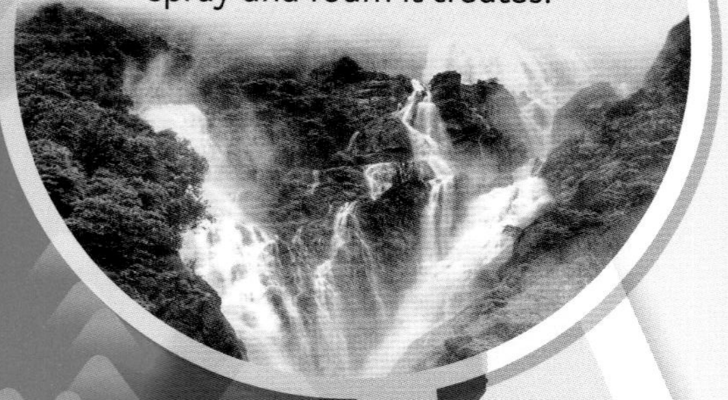

WESTERN GHATS

The fruit of this tree is used to make the state's traditional liquor, feni

SCALE

0 5 kilometers
0 5 miles

MAHARASHTRA

Valpoi

Ponda

Bicholim

Mandovi

Pernem

Chapora

Mapusa

Chimbel

Dr. Salim Ali Bird Sanctuary

Baga

Panaji

Deu boro dis dium
Good day to you

Situated on the banks of the Mandovi river, this sanctuary is known for its mangrove swamps

N E S W

ARABIAN SEA

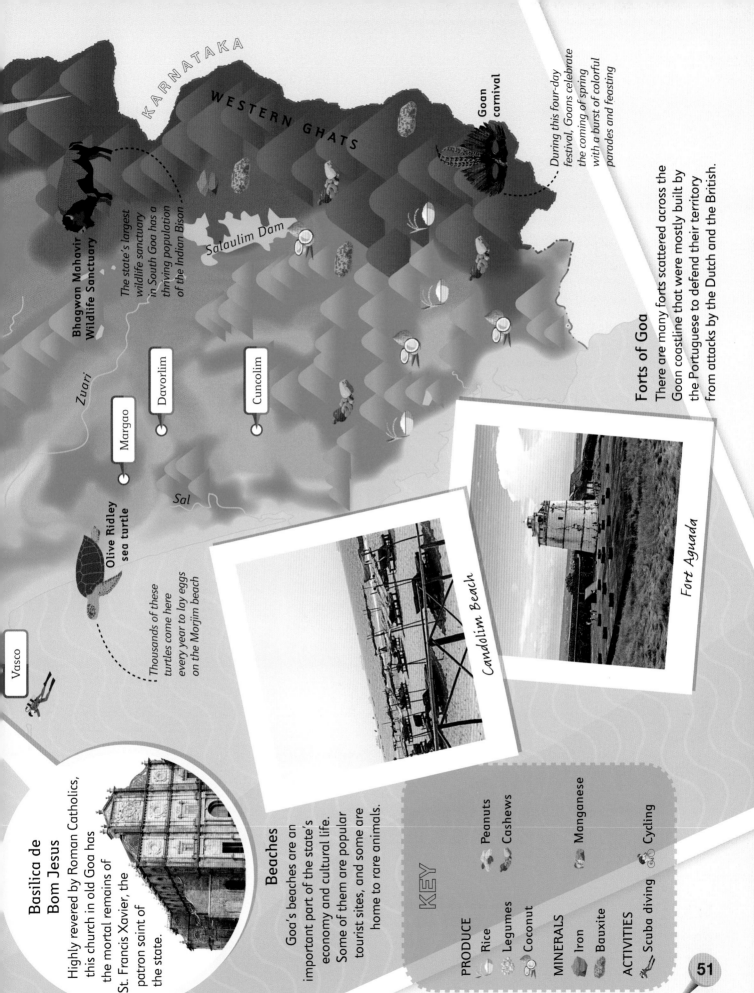

KARNATAKA

WESTERN GHATS

Goan carnival

During this four-day festival, Goans celebrate the coming of spring with a burst of colorful parades and feasting

Bhagwan Mahavir Wildlife Sanctuary

The state's largest wildlife sanctuary in South Goa has a thriving population of the Indian Bison

Salaulim Dam

Zuari

Margao

Davorlim

Cuncolim

Sal

Vasco

Olive Ridley sea turtle

Thousands of these turtles come here every year to lay eggs on the Morjim beach

Forts of Goa

There are many forts scattered across the Goan coastline that were mostly built by the Portuguese to defend their territory from attacks by the Dutch and the British.

Candolim Beach

Fort Aguada

Basilica de Bom Jesus

Highly revered by Roman Catholics, this church in old Goa has the mortal remains of St. Francis Xavier, the patron saint of the state.

Beaches

Goa's beaches are an important part of the state's economy and cultural life. Some of them are popular tourist sites, and some are home to rare animals.

KEY

PRODUCE
- Rice
- Peanuts
- Legumes
- Cashews
- Coconut

MINERALS
- Iron
- Manganese
- Bauxite

ACTIVITIES
- Scuba diving
- Cycling

51

PUNE

Earlier known as Poona, the pleasant climate and geographical coordinates made this city indispensable to the Marathas and the British. Today, Pune is the very definition of a new-age smart city, with a thriving and fast-growing industrial hub, academia, and burgeoning businesses.

ORIGIN STORY

The name "Pune" comes from the Marathi word *Punyanagari*, which means the city of virtue. The earliest mention of Pune can be traced back to 758 CE copper plates from the Rashtrakuta dynasty, which refer to it as *Punya Vishaya*, meaning a holy land.

Pune has been home to social reformers and educationalists, such as Savitribai Phule, the mother of girls' education in India, her husband Jyotirao Phule, and India's first female physician, Anandi Gopal Joshi.

FAMOUS FACES

WOW!

Pune is known as the Oxford of the East because of its countless universities and colleges.

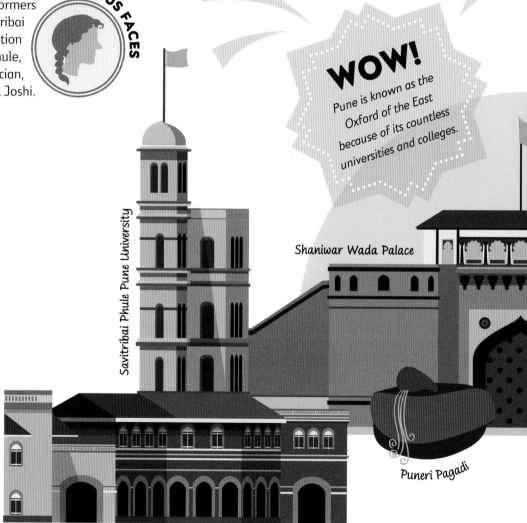

Shaniwar Wada Palace

Savitribai Phule Pune University

Puneri Pagadi

28,000

The number of ancient manuscripts housed in Bhandarkar Oriental Research Institute, Savatribai Phule Pune University.

TOP 5

1 Remains of the **Shaniwar Wada Palace,** which was the seat of power for Peshwa rulers, is located in the old city. This 18th-century fortress was destroyed in a fire in 1828, but its mighty walls and gateways still stand.

2 Many tourists visit the **OSHO International Meditation Resort,** established in 1975 by self-professed guru Rajneesh who founded a controversial religious movement.

Also known as "retirement paradise," Pune has many senior living quarters. Its greenery, open spaces, and pleasant weather offer peace and quiet, which attract many newly retired officials and military personnel.

The Sanjeev Kumar–Deven Verma film *Angoor* (1982) and Aamir Khan's *Dangal* (2016) were shot in Pune.

AGA KHAN PALACE

Commissioned in 1892 by Aga Khan III, a prominent imam, this majestic monument is known for its Italian arches. During the Quit India Movement in 1942, Kasturba, Mahatma Gandhi, and many other freedom fighters were imprisoned here. Kasturba died in the palace during this time. In 1969, it was donated to the people of India to honor Gandhi and his philosophy. His ashes are kept here.

MAD ABOUT

Learning and spirituality

DID YOU KNOW?

Pune was the capital and the center of power of the Maratha Empire. It became the monsoon capital during the British Raj.

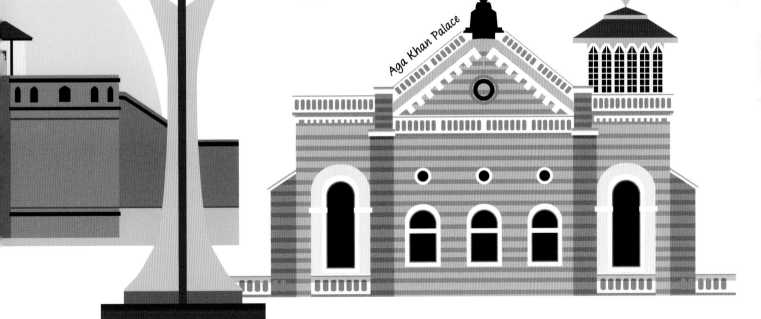

Aga Khan Palace

National War Memorial Southern Command

3 Unveiled in 1998, the **National War Memorial Southern Command** is dedicated to the martyrs of the wars fought after independence.

4 To escape the land of buildings, visit the **Pune Okayama Friendship Garden,** inspired by a 300-year-old garden in Japan.

5 The **Sinhagad Fort**, nestled on the Sahyadri, was the site of the famous battle of Sinhagad between the Marathas and the Mughal armies in 1670.

CENTRAL INDIA

Covering a vast area of nearly 250,000 sq miles (400,000 sq km), the thickly forested states of Madhya Pradesh and Chhattisgarh constitute the geographical heart of India. The region is also a rich source of mineral wealth, with Madhya Pradesh as the sole diamond-producing state in the country.

CHAMBAL RAVINES

The Chambal valley in the Vindhya range is characterized by badlands, consisting of plateaus and ravines. The region is situated at the meeting point of Rajasthan, Uttar Pradesh, and Madhya Pradesh, and is infamous for being home to some of the country's most dreaded criminals. The river Chambal, a tributary of Yamuna, flows through the region.

Gwalior Fort

ARCHITECTURE

The region's glorious history and artistic traditions are manifested in its countless temples, forts, and palaces. From the holy sites of worship at Sanchi and Bhoramdeo to the magnificent forts of Gwalior and Mandu, central India has many architectural marvels.

TRIBAL GROUPS

The two states are home to 22 percent of the country's tribal population. The Bastar district in Chhattisgarh has several tribes and communities. The craftsmen of these tribes make decorative objects out of locally available materials such as clay, wood, metal, and cotton yarn. Animals, birds, and plants are common decorations in their work.

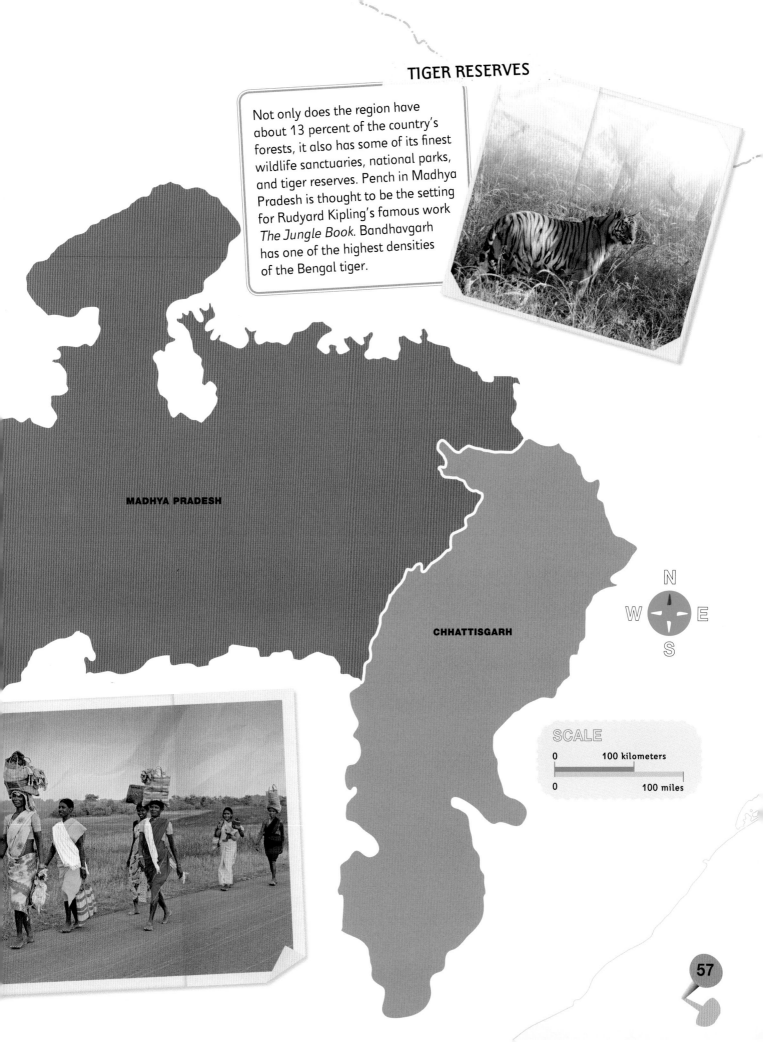

TIGER RESERVES

Not only does the region have about 13 percent of the country's forests, it also has some of its finest wildlife sanctuaries, national parks, and tiger reserves. Pench in Madhya Pradesh is thought to be the setting for Rudyard Kipling's famous work *The Jungle Book*. Bandhavgarh has one of the highest densities of the Bengal tiger.

MADHYA PRADESH

CHHATTISGARH

N
W E
S

SCALE

0   100 kilometers

0   100 miles

MADHYA PRADESH

Situated in the heart of India, Madhya Pradesh's craggy ravines and rocky hills make for a varied terrain. Its forests are home to about half of India's tiger population. From the Sanchi Stupa to the intricately carved temples of Khajuraho, the state has many architectural marvels.

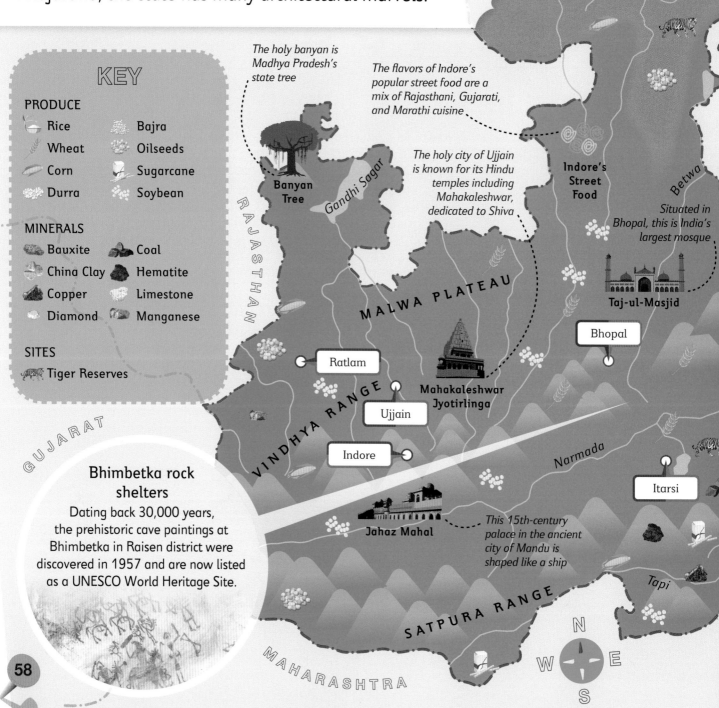

Born in Gwalior, Tansen was one of the nine gems in Akbar's court

Tansen

Chambal

Gwalior

Sind

The holy banyan is Madhya Pradesh's state tree

The flavors of Indore's popular street food are a mix of Rajasthani, Gujarati, and Marathi cuisine

The holy city of Ujjain is known for its Hindu temples including Mahakaleshwar, dedicated to Shiva

Indore's Street Food

Banyan Tree

Gandhi Sagar

Betwa

Situated in Bhopal, this is India's largest mosque

KEY

PRODUCE
- Rice
- Wheat
- Corn
- Durra
- Bajra
- Oilseeds
- Sugarcane
- Soybean

MINERALS
- Bauxite
- China Clay
- Copper
- Diamond
- Coal
- Hematite
- Limestone
- Manganese

SITES
- Tiger Reserves

RAJASTHAN

MALWA PLATEAU

Taj-ul-Masjid

Bhopal

Ratlam

Mahakaleshwar Jyotirlinga

VINDHYA RANGE

Ujjain

Indore

GUJARAT

Narmada

Itarsi

Bhimbetka rock shelters

Dating back 30,000 years, the prehistoric cave paintings at Bhimbetka in Raisen district were discovered in 1957 and are now listed as a UNESCO World Heritage Site.

Jahaz Mahal

This 15th-century palace in the ancient city of Mandu is shaped like a ship

Tapi

SATPURA RANGE

MAHARASHTRA

N
W   E
S

Kanha National Park

One of the state's largest national parks, Kanha is the only habitat of the barasingha. The park is also home to tigers, chital, leopards, and wild dogs.

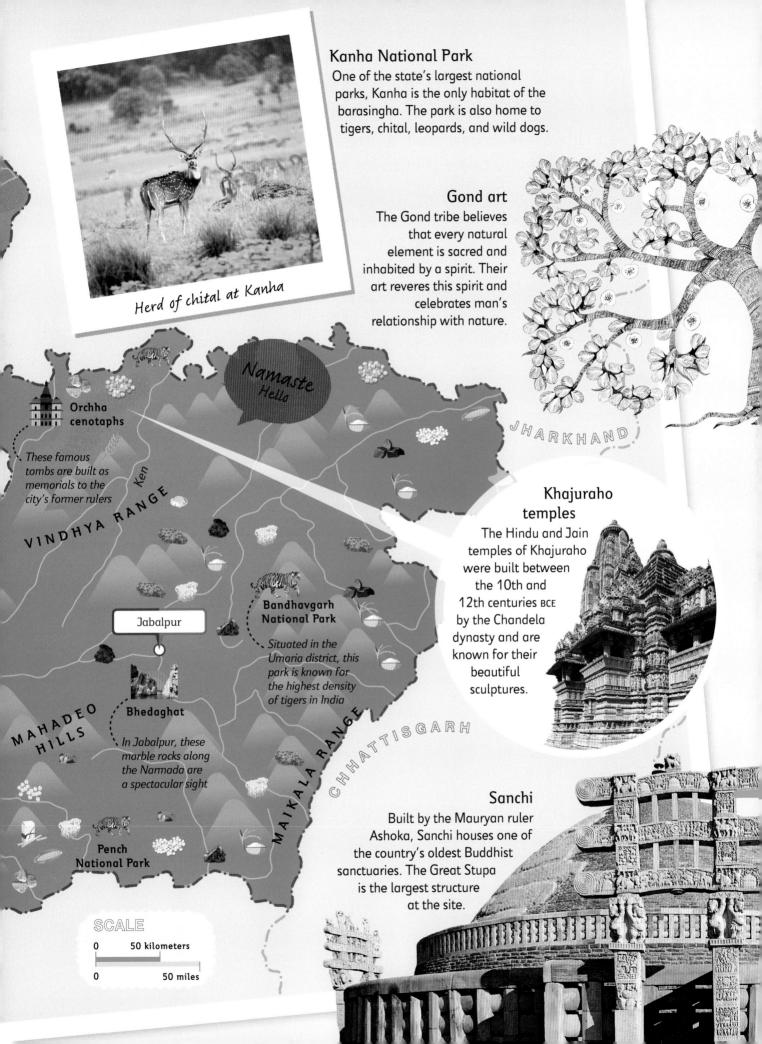

Herd of chital at Kanha

Gond art

The Gond tribe believes that every natural element is sacred and inhabited by a spirit. Their art reveres this spirit and celebrates man's relationship with nature.

Namaste
Hello

JHARKHAND

Orchha cenotaphs

These famous tombs are built as memorials to the city's former rulers

Ken

VINDHYA RANGE

Jabalpur

Bandhavgarh National Park

Situated in the Umaria district, this park is known for the highest density of tigers in India

Khajuraho temples

The Hindu and Jain temples of Khajuraho were built between the 10th and 12th centuries BCE by the Chandela dynasty and are known for their beautiful sculptures.

Bhedaghat

In Jabalpur, these marble rocks along the Narmada are a spectacular sight

MAHADEO HILLS

MAIKALA RANGE

CHHATTISGARH

Pench National Park

Sanchi

Built by the Mauryan ruler Ashoka, Sanchi houses one of the country's oldest Buddhist sanctuaries. The Great Stupa is the largest structure at the site.

SCALE

0   50 kilometers

0   50 miles

RIVER SYSTEMS

India has a vast network of large and small rivers that can be broadly classified into two—Himalayan and Peninsular—based on relief, origin, and characteristics. Whether they are perennial, seasonal, fast-flowing, calm, short, or long, rivers play a crucial role in our lives.

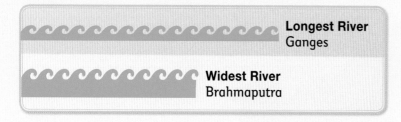

Longest River
Ganges

Widest River
Brahmaputra

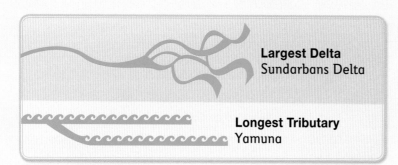

Largest Delta
Sundarbans Delta

Longest Tributary
Yamuna

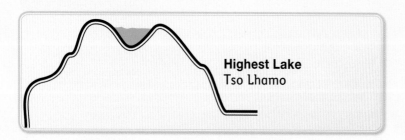

Highest Lake
Tso Lhamo

Rainfall is the primary source for Peninsular rivers

HIMALAYAN RIVERS

▸ This system consists of about 20 rivers. Indus, Ganges, and Brahmaputra are the major ones.

▸ These rivers are fed by melting snow from the Himalayas, the Trans-Himalayas, and rainfall. This is why they are considered perennial.

▸ They have long courses, from their source of origin in the Himalayas to their point of discharge, either into the Bay of Bengal or the Arabian Sea.

PENINSULAR RIVERS

▸ Narmada, Tapi, Krishna, Godavari, Mahanadi, and Kaveri are major Peninsular rivers.

▸ These rivers are mostly seasonal and dependent on rainfall.

▸ They have a comparatively shorter course. Most of the major Peninsular rivers originate in the Western Ghats and drain into the Bay of Bengal.

MODEL OF A RIVER SYSTEM

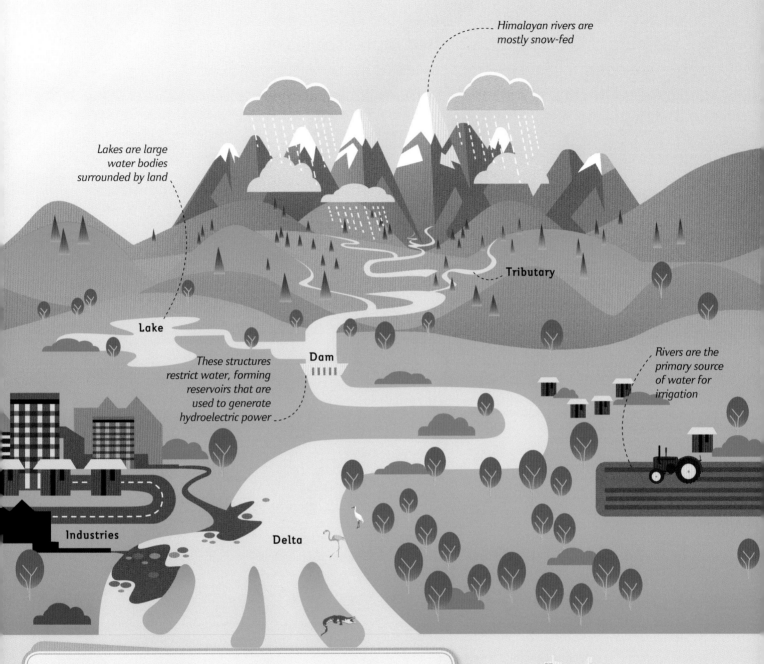

Himalayan rivers are mostly snow-fed

Lakes are large water bodies surrounded by land

Tributary

Lake

These structures restrict water, forming reservoirs that are used to generate hydroelectric power

Dam

Rivers are the primary source of water for irrigation

Industries

Delta

RIVER POLLUTION

▶ Rivers and lakes are the only freshwater source in the world, and their increasing levels of water pollution is alarming. More people die of drinking contaminated water every year than in wars or other forms of violence.

▶ Rivers are polluted by the release of untreated sewage and toxic industrial waste into the waters.

▶ Various religious rituals, such as the immersion of idols and holy baptisms in the rivers, also pollute them.

▶ River pollution not only makes the water unfit for drinking, but also damages the habitat of marine animals and plants, endangering the ecosystem.

61

CHHATTISGARH

Carved out of Madhya Pradesh in November 2000, the thickly forested state of Chhattisgarh is blessed with unspoiled and unexplored natural beauty—from cascading waterfalls to wildlife sanctuaries. The state is also home to many tribes who create some of the finest crafts in the country.

Namaste
Hello

Nilgai

Gomarda Sanctuary

The vast grasslands of Gomarda in the Raigarh district shelter many animals, including nilgai, bison, and spotted deer.

This ancient Shiva temple in the Kabirdham district was built by King Ramchandra of the Nag dynasty

Bhoramdeo Temple

MAIKALA RANGE

Bhilai

Rajnandgaon

Durg

Raipur

Wrought iron

Artisans craft figurines and lamps in wrought iron using technique called Loha Shilp

MAHARASHTRA

This sanctuary in the Bijapur district is home to one of the last populations of the wild buffalo

These ancient caves in Bastar have formations of stalactites and stalagmites, some of which are worshipped

Kailash and Kutumsar caves

Pairi

Chitrakote Falls

At almost 1,000 ft (300 m), Chitrakote is considered India's widest waterfall. It cascades about 100 ft down to the Indravati river near Jagdalpur in the Bastar district.

BASTAR HILLS

Indravati National Sanctuary

Indravati

Kanger Valley National Park

This park is known for its stunning waterfalls and limestone caves

Gaur Maria

The hunting tribe of Bastar performs this dance on special occasions such as weddings

TELENGANA

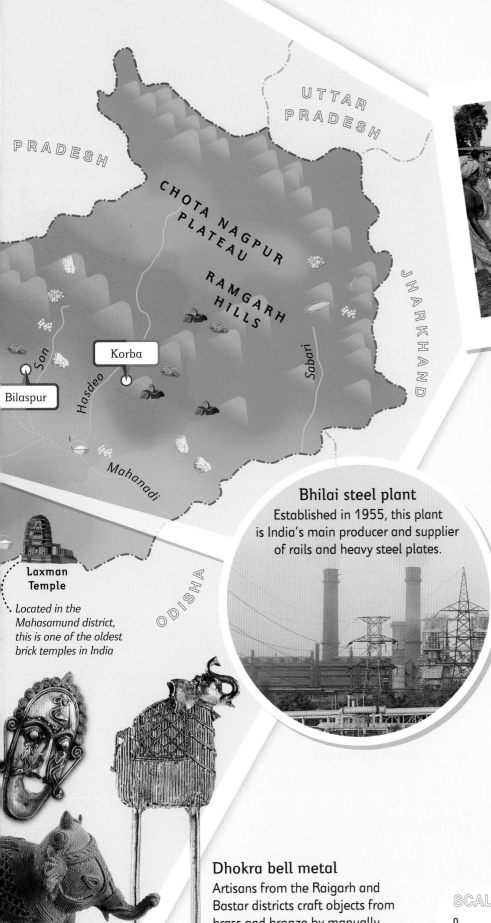

PRADESH

UTTAR PRADESH

CHOTA NAGPUR PLATEAU

RAMGARH HILLS

JHARKHAND

Son

Hasdeo

Korba

Bilaspur

Sabari

Mahanadi

ODISHA

Laxman Temple

Located in the Mahasamund district, this is one of the oldest brick temples in India

Tribal markets in Bastar

Bastar

This district is predominantly inhabited by tribal groups, many of whom avoid contact with outsiders to preserve their unique culture. Each tribe has its own costume, customs, traditions, and forms of worship. They are known for their craftsmanship and are considered among the earliest to have worked with metal.

Bhilai steel plant

Established in 1955, this plant is India's main producer and supplier of rails and heavy steel plates.

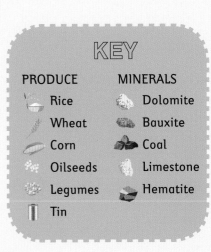

KEY	
PRODUCE	**MINERALS**
Rice	Dolomite
Wheat	Bauxite
Corn	Coal
Oilseeds	Limestone
Legumes	Hematite
Tin	

Dhokra bell metal

Artisans from the Raigarh and Bastar districts craft objects from brass and bronze by manually casting them with the help of wax—a centuries-old technique.

SCALE

0   50 kilometers

0   50 miles

NORTHEAST INDIA

The northeast region comprises seven states known as the "Seven Sisters," and is linked to the rest of the country by a narrow strip of land. This relative isolation gives a distinctive quality to the lifestyle and culture of the area, which has diverse ethnic groups, languages, religions, and landscapes.

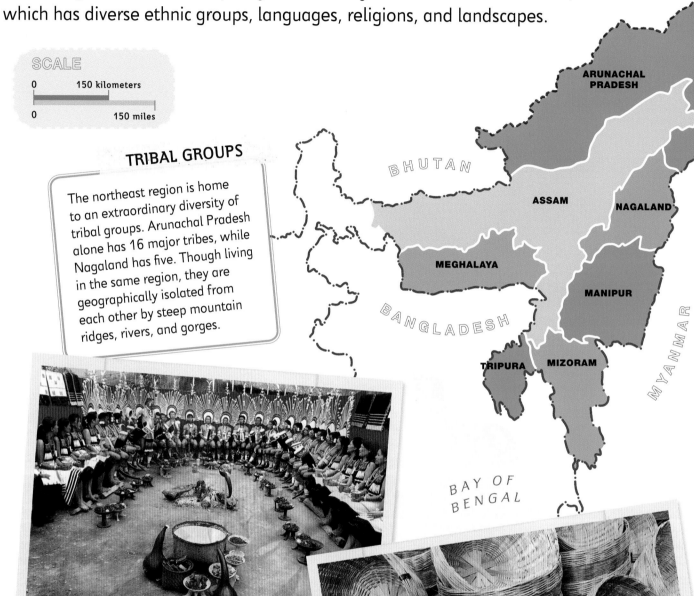

SCALE

0   150 kilometers

0   150 miles

BHUTAN

ARUNACHAL PRADESH

ASSAM

NAGALAND

MEGHALAYA

MANIPUR

BANGLADESH

TRIPURA   MIZORAM

MYANMAR

BAY OF BENGAL

TRIBAL GROUPS

The northeast region is home to an extraordinary diversity of tribal groups. Arunachal Pradesh alone has 16 major tribes, while Nagaland has five. Though living in the same region, they are geographically isolated from each other by steep mountain ridges, rivers, and gorges.

Almost 64 percent of the country's bamboo grows in this region and, as a result, bamboo craft is a vital part of the states' economy. Artisans have been practicing the craft for centuries. They use bamboo to create a wide variety of products, ranging from furniture and fences, to baskets and hats.

BAMBOO CRAFT

TEA PLANTATIONS

Northeast states, such as Assam, Tripura, and Meghalaya, are major tea-growing areas. Assam accounts for approximately 50 percent of India's total output of tea. The state benefits from rich soil and monsoon rains, making it the most productive tea-growing region in the world.

WILDLIFE SANCTUARIES

These thickly forested states have a plethora of wildlife sanctuaries and national parks. They provide shelter to several species of endangered fauna, such as the Indian rhinoceros, the red panda, and the hoolock gibbon.

Manas National Park, Assam

BRAHMAPUTRA

The majestic Brahmaputra river dominates life in Assam and much of Arunachal Pradesh. It begins its long journey from the holy mountain of Kailasa in Tibet, then enters the plains near the Assam-Arunachal border and flows westward. It is broad and tranquil, except during the monsoon season when it swells enormously, causing floods in the Assam valley almost annually.

NATURAL WONDERS

A treasure trove of diverse topography, India has it all—from fragrant high altitude meadows in the north and a massive crater lake in the west, to a disappearing sea in the east and a mud volcano in the south.

The water of the Umngot river that flows through the town of Dawki in Meghalaya is so clear and clean that from land, boats seem to be floating in midair!

FOSSIL PARKS

Fossilized trees are rare. They can be found in only a few parts of the world.

SIWALIK FOSSIL PARK,
Himachal Pradesh

This park is home to one of the richest collections of fossils belonging to mammals who roamed the earth almost 2.5 million years ago such as a hipopolamid, a large-tusked elephant, a gharial, a four-horned giraffe, and a saber-toothed cat.

NATIONAL FOSSIL WOOD PARK, Tamil Nadu

About 200 fossil trees, dating back almost 20 million years, have been preserved here. The recovered fossilized remains have their tree rings intact, giving a glimpse into what the flora was like back then.

ISLANDS

MAJULI ISLAND,
Assam

The largest inhabited river island in the world, Majuli Island is located on the Brahmaputra river. It is home to almost 160,000 people, who live in wooden-stilted houses, and a far larger population of goats, cows, and pigs.

ST MARY'S ISLANDS,
Karnataka

This group of islands is known for the rare hexagonal, basaltic rock columns on its shores. Geological studies have revealed that these islands have existed from the time Madagascar and Africa separated from India.

WATER BODIES

LOKTAK LAKE,
Manipur

At first glance, this large lake seems like it is covered with micro-islands. These are, in fact, *phumdis*, or floating masses of vegetation, decomposing organic matter, and soil. This is also the home of the endangered dancing deer and the world's only floating national park.

LONAR CRATER LAKE,
Maharashtra

One of India's meteorite craters, this lake was created as a result of an impact that took place almost 50,000 years ago on volcanic basalt rock. It has a depth of almost 500 ft (150 m) and a diameter of 6,000 ft (1,830 m).

FALLS

HOGENAKKAL FALLS,
Karnataka and Tamil Nadu

With its origins in Karnataka, the Kaveri river flows through the Tamil Nadu border. At the meeting point of the two states, the river splits into many streams that descend over a rocky gorge as a waterfall.

NOHKALIKAI FALLS,
Meghalaya

At a height of 1,115 ft (340 m), this is the tallest plunge waterfall in India. The water falls into a pool, which has a peculiar green color. The name comes from the tragic story of a woman called Ka Likai who jumped from the gorge.

MOUNTAINS

VALLEY OF FLOWERS NATIONAL PARK, Uttarakhand

A delight for hikers and botanists, this UNESCO World Heritage Site is known for its scenic meadows of alpine flowers. It is also home to many endangered animals such as the Asiatic black bear and snow leopard.

DID YOU KNOW?

Twice a day, the sea level on Odisha's Hide and Seek Beach recedes as far back as 3 miles (5 km) during low tide, making it disappear. The sea returns at high tide.

Defying gravity

About 20 miles (30 km) away from the town of Leh, the laws of gravity do not apply. When parked at a certain spot on the mysterious Magnetic Hill, a parked car seems to move forward at a speed of about 12 mph (20 kph). Many believe the hill has magnetic properties, but it's actually just an optical illusion.

DID YOU KNOW?

High wind pressure during the monsoon season creates a reverse waterfall, which can be seen along the Western Ghats close to Sinhagad Fort in Maharashtra.

BARREN ISLAND,
Andaman and Nicobar Islands

Home to the only active volcano in India, this island lies on the India and Burma plate. As its name suggests, it is a barren area where no humans live. Its only residents are goats, birds, bats, flying foxes, and rodents that can survive the region's severe, uninhabitable conditions caused by occasional eruptions. A special permit is needed to visit this island.

MUD VOLCANOES,
Andaman and Nicobar Islands

The only mud volcanoes in India, they occur because of underground gas emissions mixed with rocks and mud. Unlike igneous volcanoes that spew lava, these have mud or slurries that ooze and spill over the edges.

69

ARUNACHAL PRADESH

Situated on the northeastern edge of India, Arunachal Pradesh shares international borders with Bhutan, China, and Myanmar. It is the first state in the country to see the sun rise. The state's landscape has dense forests, deep valleys, steep hills, and lofty mountains.

Masked dancers

Torgya
This three-day festival symbolizes the destruction of evil and the ushering in of peace and prosperity. It is only celebrated in the Tawang Monastery. Monks wear brightly colored animal masks for the dance.

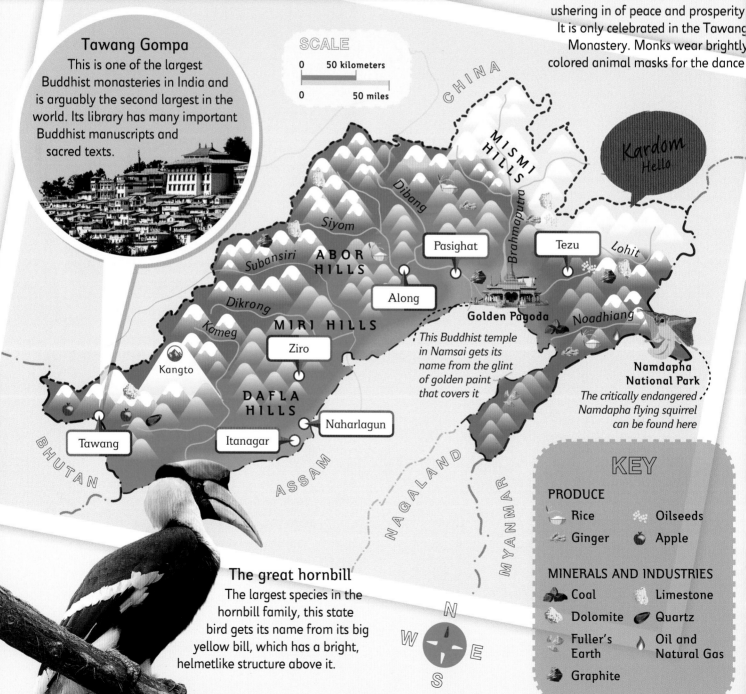

Tawang Gompa
This is one of the largest Buddhist monasteries in India and is arguably the second largest in the world. Its library has many important Buddhist manuscripts and sacred texts.

SCALE
0   50 kilometers
0   50 miles

CHINA

MISMI HILLS

Kardom
Hello

Dibang

Siyom

Subansiri

ABOR HILLS

Pasighat

Brahmaputra

Tezu

Lohit

Along

Dikrong

Golden Pagoda

Noadhiang

Kameg

MIRI HILLS

Ziro

This Buddhist temple in Namsai gets its name from the glint of golden paint that covers it

Namdapha National Park
The critically endangered Namdapha flying squirrel can be found here

Kangto

DAFLA HILLS

Naharlagun

Tawang   Itanagar

BHUTAN

ASSAM

NAGALAND

MYANMAR

The great hornbill
The largest species in the hornbill family, this state bird gets its name from its big yellow bill, which has a bright, helmetlike structure above it.

N W E S

KEY

PRODUCE
- Rice
- Oilseeds
- Ginger
- Apple

MINERALS AND INDUSTRIES
- Coal
- Limestone
- Dolomite
- Quartz
- Fuller's Earth
- Oil and Natural Gas
- Graphite

Arts and crafts

Nagaland's tribes are known for their fine craft skills, especially woodcarving and jewelry made with beads and shells. Woodcraft is traditionally practiced by men.

Angami jewelry

Woodcarving

Kinika ase
How are you?

Kachari ruins

These 13th-century ruins are in Dimapur. The site has well-preserved structures, such as temples and reservoirs, made out of massive stones.

KEY

PRODUCE

Rice   Sugarcane

Pineapple   Millet

Corn   Potato

MINERALS

Coal   Limestone

Magnetite

ASSAM

Dikhu

Mon

MYANMAR

Teunsang

NAGA HILLS

This national park in Peren district was declared an elephant reserve in 2005

Dimapur

Kohima

Phek

Intanki National Park

Kohima War Cemetery

This cemetery has the graves of 1,400 Indian, British, and Commonwealth soldiers who died in World War II

N W E S

MANIPUR

SCALE

0   25 kilometers

0   25 miles

NAGALAND

Almost all of Nagaland is mountainous, with the Naga Hills covering the state entirely. One-sixth of it is forested. It was formally declared a state of India in 1963. It is home to more than 20 tribes that mostly live in isolated villages.

Hornbill festival

All Naga tribes participate in this seven-day festival, which is held in Kohima. It is organized by the government to showcase the state's cultural diversity.

ASSAM

Dominated by India's widest river, the mighty Brahmaputra, Assam is considered to be the gateway to northeastern India. It shares its borders with the other six states in the region. It is known for its lush forests, fertile lands, rich tea gardens, the Indian rhinoceros, and warm, friendly people.

Kamakhya Temple
Dedicated to the mother goddess, this Hindu temple does not house idols or images. Instead, a symbol of the yoni is worshipped here.

Rongali Bihu
The festival marks the Assamese New Year and is celebrated with lively singing, drumming, and dancing. Celebrated in the month of April, the festival marks the beginning of the harvest season.

Situated in the Baksa district, this sanctuary is home to a variety of animals, such as the Indian elephant

BHUTAN

Tezpur

Manas National Park

Manas

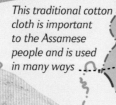

Bihu dance

This traditional cotton cloth is important to the Assamese people and is used in many ways

Gamosa

Brahmaputra

Guwahati — Dispur

MEGHALAYA

Nomoskar
Hello

SCALE
0   50 kilometers

0   50 miles

BANGLADESH

Kaziranga National Park
A UNESCO World Heritage Site, Kaziranga, in the Golaghat and Nagaon districts, is one of the last refuges of the greater one-horned rhinoceros.

TRIPURA

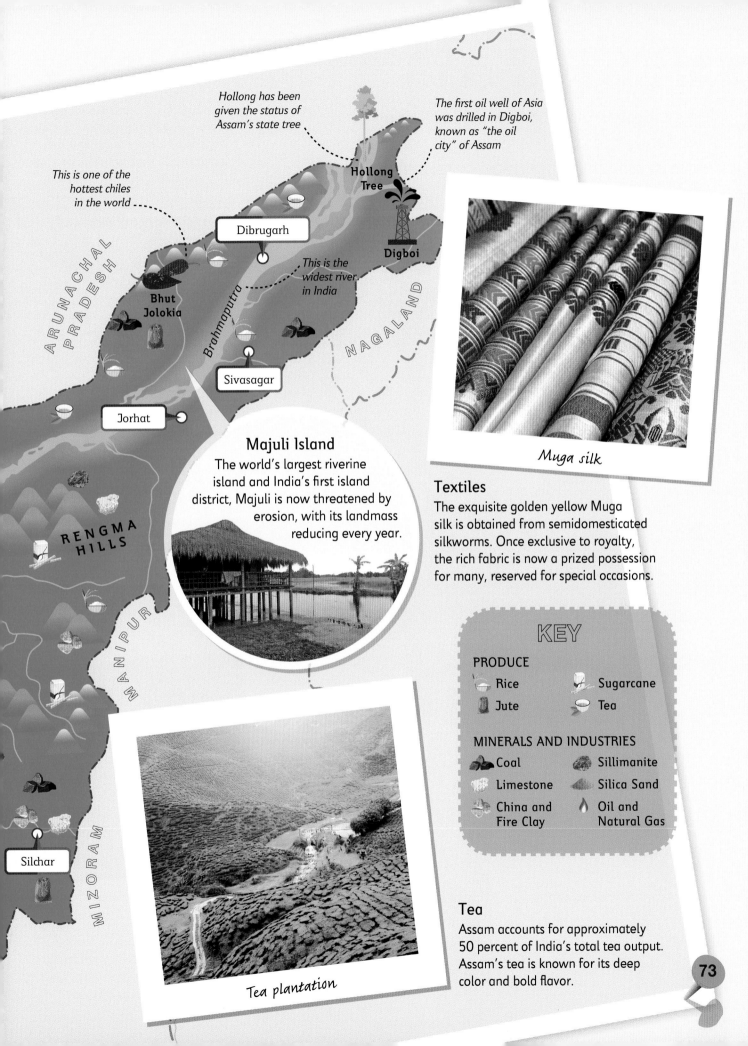

Hollong has been given the status of Assam's state tree

The first oil well of Asia was drilled in Digboi, known as "the oil city" of Assam

This is one of the hottest chiles in the world

Hollong Tree

Digboi

Dibrugarh

ARUNACHAL PRADESH

Bhut Jolokia

Brahmaputra

This is the widest river in India

NAGALAND

Sivasagar

Jorhat

Majuli Island
The world's largest riverine island and India's first island district, Majuli is now threatened by erosion, with its landmass reducing every year.

RENGMA HILLS

MANIPUR

MIZORAM

Silchar

Muga silk

Textiles
The exquisite golden yellow Muga silk is obtained from semidomesticated silkworms. Once exclusive to royalty, the rich fabric is now a prized possession for many, reserved for special occasions.

KEY

PRODUCE

Rice

Sugarcane

Jute

Tea

MINERALS AND INDUSTRIES

Coal

Sillimanite

Limestone

Silica Sand

China and Fire Clay

Oil and Natural Gas

Tea plantation

Tea
Assam accounts for approximately 50 percent of India's total tea output. Assam's tea is known for its deep color and bold flavor.

MEGHALAYA

Meghalaya means "abode of clouds," an apt phrase considering the state has the world's wettest region, Mawsynram. The village receives an annual rainfall of more than 450 inches (11,400 mm). The state also has the Garo, Khasi, and Jaintia hills, named after the tribes that form the majority of its population.

Root bridges

The Khasis have devised a unique way of crossing overflowing rivers during the monsoon—living root bridges. The roots of rubber trees are connected across the rivers, which turn into strong bridges over time.

Clouded Leopard

The state animal is named for the cloud-shaped markings on its body. Its population is severely threatened because of poaching and habitat loss.

This reserve in West Garo Hills protects the endangered western hoolock gibbon

This museum in Shillong has a large collection of insects, such as moths, beetles, and butterflies

Located in the Jaintia hills, it is the longest natural cave in the country

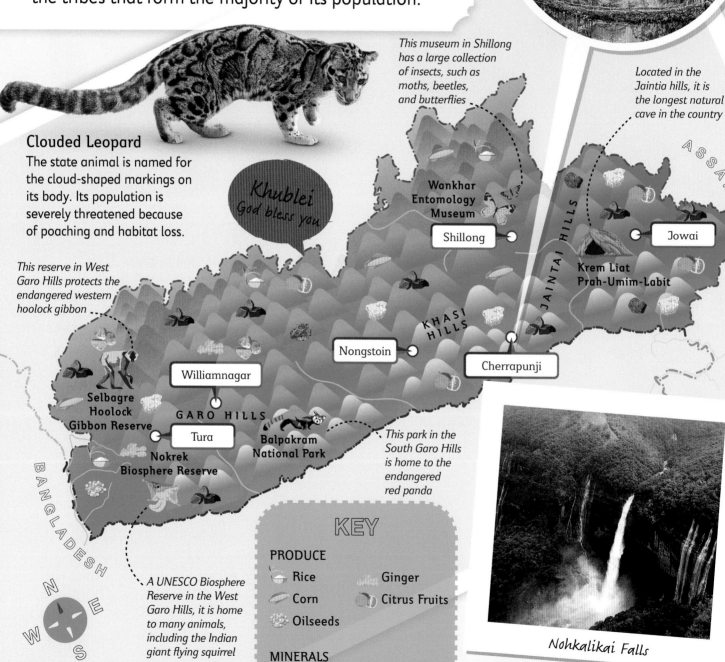

Khublei
God bless you

ASSAM

Wankhar Entomology Museum

Shillong

JAINTIA HILLS

Jowai

Krem Liat Prah-Umim-Labit

KHASI HILLS

Nongstoin

Cherrapunji

Selbagre Hoolock Gibbon Reserve

GARO HILLS

Williamnagar

Tura

Nokrek Biosphere Reserve

Balpakram National Park

This park in the South Garo Hills is home to the endangered red panda

BANGLADESH

A UNESCO Biosphere Reserve in the West Garo Hills, it is home to many animals, including the Indian giant flying squirrel

N
W E
S

KEY

PRODUCE
- Rice
- Corn
- Oilseeds
- Ginger
- Citrus Fruits

MINERALS
- Coal
- Limestone
- Apatite
- Sillimanite
- China Clay

Nohkalikai Falls

Waterfalls

The state has many spectacular waterfalls. The Nohkalikai Falls in Cherrapunji is particularly dramatic during the monsoon season, when its capacity increases as much as 20 times.

SCALE

0   25 kilometers

0   25 miles

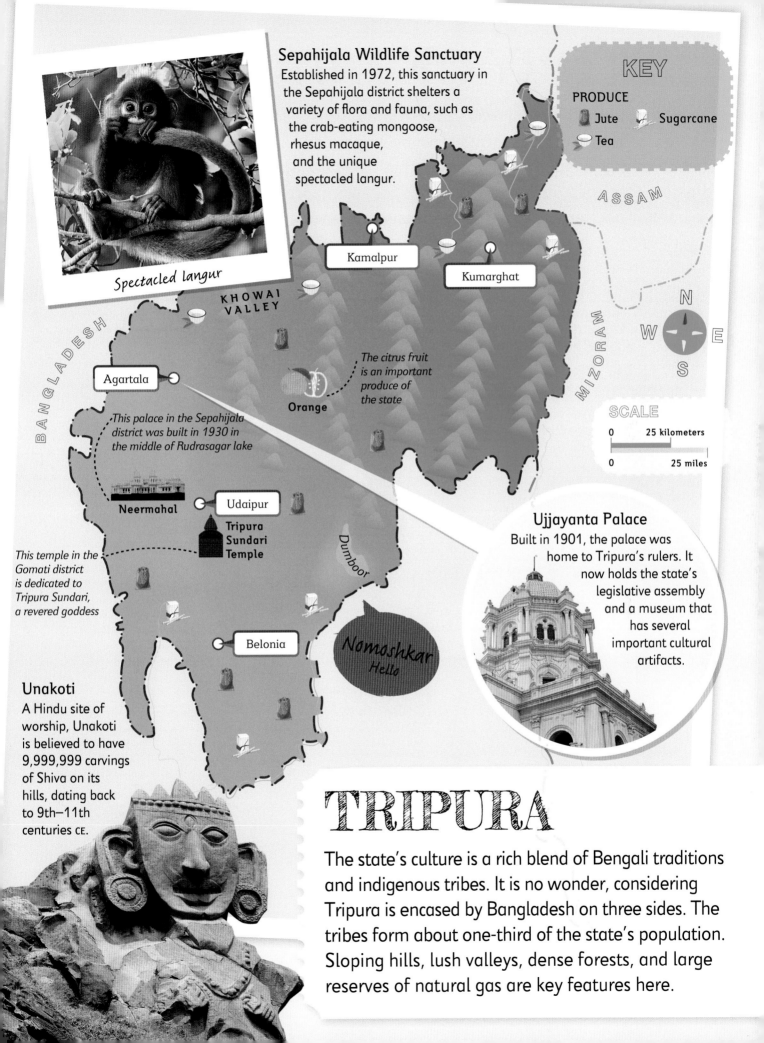

Sepahijala Wildlife Sanctuary

Established in 1972, this sanctuary in the Sepahijala district shelters a variety of flora and fauna, such as the crab-eating mongoose, rhesus macaque, and the unique spectacled langur.

Spectacled langur

KEY
PRODUCE
Jute   Sugarcane
Tea

ASSAM

KHOWAI VALLEY

Kamalpur

Kumarghat

BANGLADESH

MIZORAM

N
W   E
S

Agartala

The citrus fruit is an important produce of the state

Orange

This palace in the Sepahijala district was built in 1930 in the middle of Rudrasagar lake

SCALE

0   25 kilometers

0   25 miles

Neermahal

Udaipur

Tripura Sundari Temple

Dumboor

This temple in the Gomati district is dedicated to Tripura Sundari, a revered goddess

Ujjayanta Palace

Built in 1901, the palace was home to Tripura's rulers. It now holds the state's legislative assembly and a museum that has several important cultural artifacts.

Belonia

Nomoshkar
Hello

Unakoti

A Hindu site of worship, Unakoti is believed to have 9,999,999 carvings of Shiva on its hills, dating back to 9th–11th centuries CE.

TRIPURA

The state's culture is a rich blend of Bengali traditions and indigenous tribes. It is no wonder, considering Tripura is encased by Bangladesh on three sides. The tribes form about one-third of the state's population. Sloping hills, lush valleys, dense forests, and large reserves of natural gas are key features here.

HISTORY OF INDIA

The Indian subcontinent is home to some of the richest and most diverse civilizations. The country's timeline is speckled with ruins of empires and kingdoms—great and small, indigenous and foreign—that have risen, expanded, and fallen, impacting the borders and territories of the country we call India.

The First Civilization

The Indus Valley stretched across parts of Pakistan to northwest India. It is known for being one of the most sophisticated civilizations of its time. Carefully planned cities, highly skilled water management, terra-cotta figurines, and seals are the hallmarks of this period.

Terra-cotta figurines

2500 BCE

Mughal Marvel, Taj Mahal

The Mughal Empire

A powerful and influential dynasty, the Mughals—Babur, Humayun, Akbar, Jehangir, Shah Jahan, and Aurangzeb—ruled for more than 300 years over an empire that stretched across modern Pakistan and India. Under Mughal rule, economy, literature, architecture, and the arts reached new heights.

The rulers of the Khilji dynasty (1290–1320), who came from Afghanistan, included Alauddin Khilji, a ruthless leader known for his strict control over the economy.

The Tughluqs from modern Turkey ruled from 1320 to 1414. Ghiyas-ud-din Tughlaq laid the foundation of the dynasty.

The Lodi Dynasty, which had Pashtun origins, ruled from 1451–1526. Ibrahim Lodi was the last sultan of Delhi.

The Delhi Sultanate

The armies of Muhammad Ghori from modern-day Afghanistan invaded Delhi in 1193 and laid the foundation for the Mamluk dynasty. After his death in 1206, his heir, Qutb-ud-din Aibak, became the first sultan of Delhi. The empire expanded across north India, Pakistan, and West Bengal.

Qutb Minar

1526–1707 CE

1206–1526 CE

European Settlements

Trading groups from France, the Netherlands, Portugal, and Great Britain came to India in search of cotton, spices, silk, salt, and indigo. They fought many wars against one another and the Indian rulers. The East India Company (EIC) under the British gained commercial and political control.

British Raj

Administrative rights of the EIC were annulled after the revolt of 1857 and taken over by the crown of England, controlling an empire that included modern-day India, Pakistan, Bangladesh, and Burma.

Independent India

The Partition of India took place on August 14 and East Pakistan (modern Bangladesh) and West Pakistan were created. The following day, at the stroke of midnight, India became independent, bringing together more than 560 princely states.

A struggle for independence ensued among Indians to be free from the 200-year-long British regime.

British Queen Victoria

The Indian flag

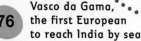

Vasco da Gama, the first European to reach India by sea

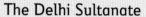

1605–1857 CE

1858–1947 CE

1947 CE

The Gangetic Civilization

The Aryans, who came to the region 1,000 years ago, extended their settlements, called Mahajanapadas, across the Gangetic Valley. Out of the 16 Mahajanapadas, the kingdom of Magadha rose to dominance and was significant even in later centuries.

An Aryan soldier

The Mauryan Empire

Also known as the first empire, it was founded by Chandragupta Maurya, the ruler of Magadha. Ashoka, his grandson, became one of India's greatest rulers, whose reign expanded from parts of present-day Pakistan to West Bengal and Kashmir to Karnataka. After his death, the empire disintegrated into smaller empires.

Lion capital of Ashoka

1500 BCE

321–185 BCE

Medieval India

The north was the focus of conflict between the Pratiharas (in central India), Rashtrakutas (in the west), and Palas (in the east). In the south, the Chalukyas declined, while the Cholas, a kingdom from the time of the Mauryan Empire, began to reassert their power.

A Chola bronze statue

The Gupta Empire

After a century, kingdoms were united under Chandragupta I. The Gupta Empire expanded from the Hindu Kush to the Himalayan mountains. Chandragupta II encouraged trade with the Arabs, China, and Europe. This period was called the golden age because of its exquisite sculptures, music, literature, and art.

Gupta-period sculpture

700–1000 CE

320–550 CE

1947 Onward

In 1956, the States Reorganization Act was passed, a reform which further classified and set boundaries of 14 states and six union territories based on linguistic lines.

1950s

On November 1, 1956, the states of Assam, Andhra Pradesh, Bihar, Jammu and Kashmir, Kerala, Madhya Pradesh, Orissa (now Odisha), Rajasthan, Punjab, and West Bengal were formed.

1960s

In 1960, the states of Maharashtra and Gujarat came into being. Goa and Nagaland became states in 1961 and 1963, respectively. The Punjab Reorganization Act created Haryana in 1966.

1970s

Himachal Pradesh became a state in 1971 and the northeastern states of Manipur and Meghalaya were formed in 1972.

2000 Onward

The new states of Uttarakhand, Chhattisgarh, and Jharkhand were formed in 2000, and Telangana in 2014.

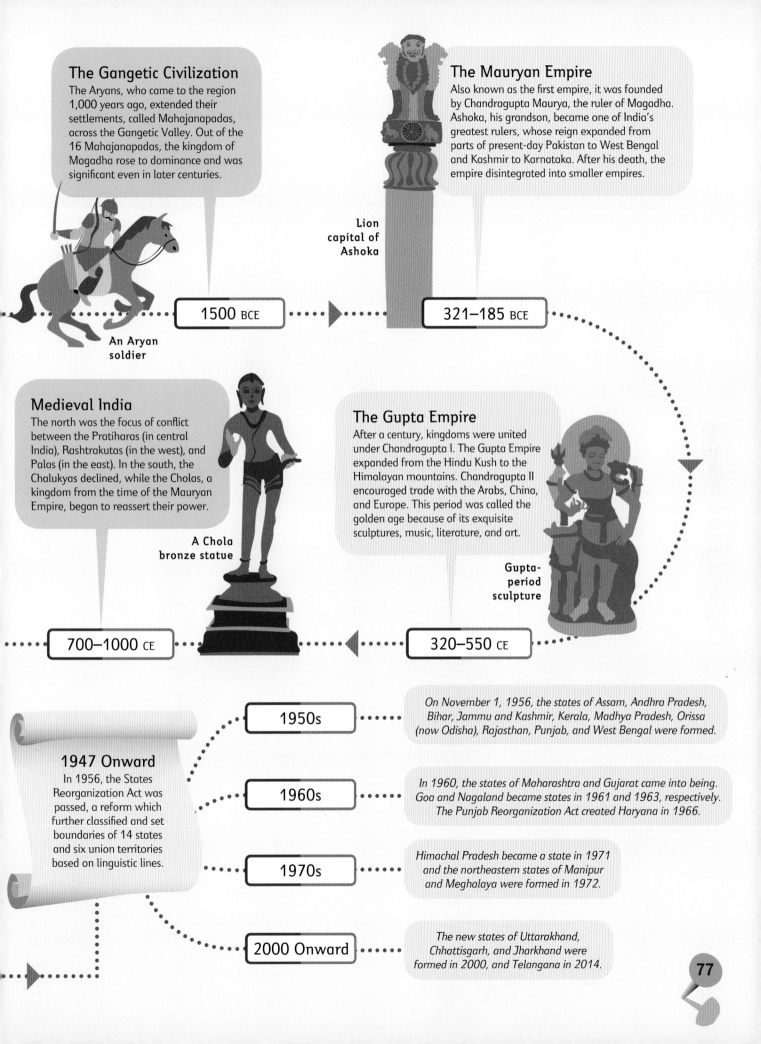

MANIPUR

The emerald-green hills and valleys of the state bear testimony to its name, which means the "land of jewels." The floating vegetation on Loktak lake provides shelter to many rare and endangered animals. Most people depend on agriculture for their livelihood.

Floating vegetation

Loktak lake
Northeast India's largest lake, Loktak is also called the world's only floating lake because of *phumdi*, masses of vegetation and soil, floating on its surface.

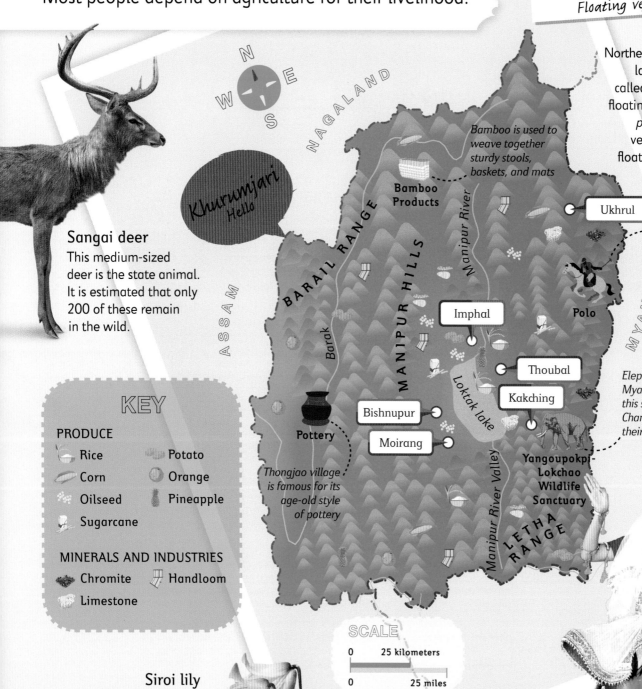

Bamboo is used to weave together sturdy stools, baskets, and mats

Khurumjari Hello

NAGALAND

ASSAM

BARAIL RANGE

Barak

MANIPUR HILLS

Manipur River

Bamboo Products

Ukhrul

This game is believed to have originated in Manipur

Polo

MYANMAR

Imphal

Thoubal

Kakching

Loktak lake

Elephants from Myanmar move to this sanctuary in the Chandel district during their seasonal migration

Bishnupur

Moirang

Pottery

Thongjao village is famous for its age-old style of pottery

Manipur River Valley

Yangoupokpi Lokchao Wildlife Sanctuary

LETHA RANGE

Sangai deer
This medium-sized deer is the state animal. It is estimated that only 200 of these remain in the wild.

KEY

PRODUCE
- Rice
- Corn
- Oilseed
- Sugarcane
- Potato
- Orange
- Pineapple

MINERALS AND INDUSTRIES
- Chromite
- Limestone
- Handloom

SCALE

| 0 | 25 kilometers |
| 0 | 25 miles |

Siroi lily
These rare flowers are found in the upper reaches of the Siroi Hills and are native to the state.

Manipuri dance
The elaborate costume of this devotional dance consists of a stiff skirt, a velvet blouse, and a white muslin cloth.

78

Chibai
Hello

KEY

MINERALS
Rice
Sugarcane
Corn

INDUSTRY
Hard Rock
Builing Material

Murlen National Park

Established as a national park in 1991, Murlen in Champhai district supports several threatened species of flora and fauna, including the state bird, Mrs. Hume's Pheasant.

TRIPURA

MANIPUR

MIZO HILLS

MYANMAR

BANGLADESH

Kolasib

This church in Aizwal is modelled after its namesake in Jerusalem

Solomon's Temple

This is the biggest wildlife sanctuary in the state

Dampa Tiger Reserve

Aizwal

Champhai

Tuival

Serchhip

Lunglei

Tlawng

Phawngpui

Lwangtlai

Saiha

Bamboo

The highest peak in Mizoram stands at a height of 7,076 ft (2,157 m)

More than 57 percent of the state is covered in bamboo forests

SCALE
0   25 kilometers
0   25 miles

N W E S

Cheraw

Dance

Mizo people have many dances, such as Cheraw and Khuallam, which are performed during festivities. In Cheraw, men sit face to face, moving long pairs of bamboo poles in rhythmic beats. Women have to step in and out of these poles.

MIZORAM

This lush, green state is one of the most sparsely populated regions in India with almost three-fourths of its surface covered in dense forests. Mizoram's population is made up of mainly tribes, and Christianity is the predominant religion.

Handicrafts

Bamboo plays an important role in the state, especially in its handicrafts. The craftsmanship is best displayed in the different types of baskets made here.

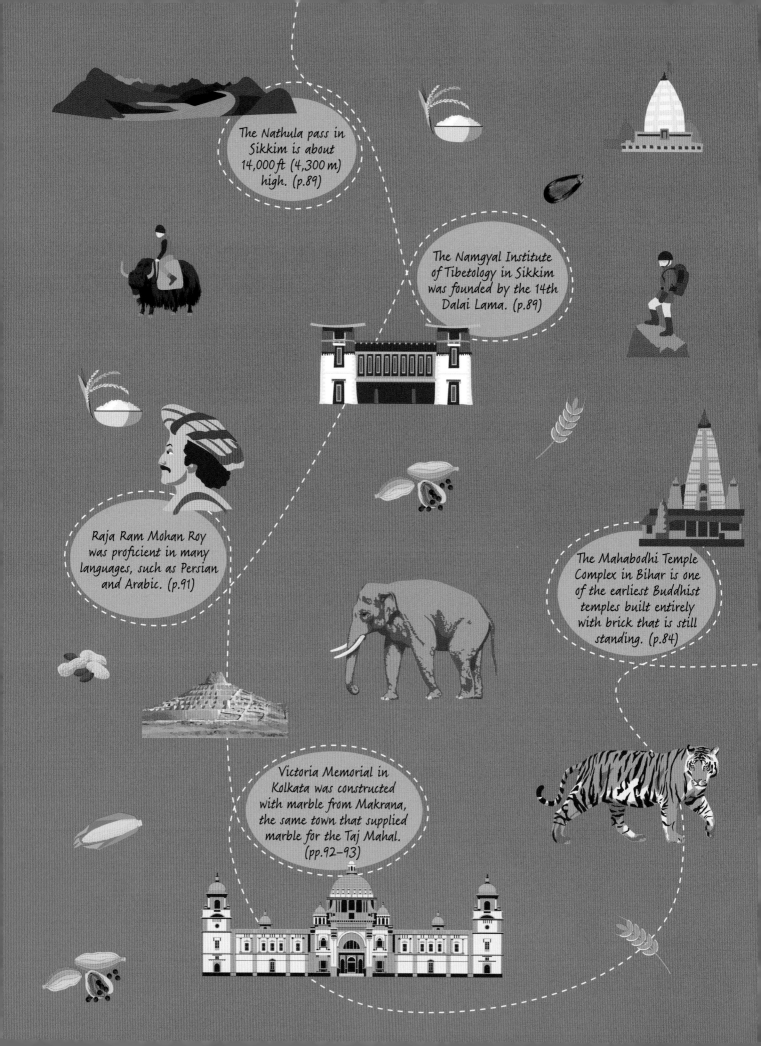

The Nathula pass in Sikkim is about 14,000 ft (4,300 m) high. (p.89)

The Namgyal Institute of Tibetology in Sikkim was founded by the 14th Dalai Lama. (p.89)

Raja Ram Mohan Roy was proficient in many languages, such as Persian and Arabic. (p.91)

The Mahabodhi Temple Complex in Bihar is one of the earliest Buddhist temples built entirely with brick that is still standing. (p.84)

Victoria Memorial in Kolkata was constructed with marble from Makrana, the same town that supplied marble for the Taj Mahal. (pp.92–93)

EAST INDIA

From the high peaks of Sikkim, mangrove forests of Bengal, and early centers of learning in Bihar, to the glorious temples of Odisha and the wealth of minerals in Jharkhand, the eastern states are rich in both natural and man-made marvels.

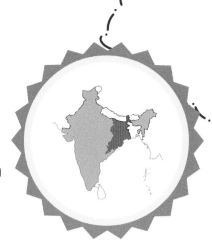

BODH GAYA

One of the holiest Buddhist sites, Bodh Gaya in Bihar is home to the Mahabodhi Temple Complex. It is here that Gautama Buddha attained enlightenment under the Bodhi tree. Mauryan emperor Ashoka established a shrine here in the 3rd century BCE.

CHOTA NAGPUR PLATEAU

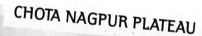

Covering most of Jharkhand, as well as parts of Odisha, Bihar, and West Bengal, the undulating Chota Nagpur Plateau covers an area of more than 40,000 sq miles (65,000 sq km). The highland is not only scenic and forested, but is rich in mineral resources and provides ore for the production of iron and steel.

Established in 1881, the Darjeeling Himalayan Railroad, commonly known as the Toy Train, was the first mountain railroad system of India. Today, it is listed on the UNESCO World Heritage List. Steam locomotives continue to operate on this line.

DARJEELING HIMALAYAN RAILROAD

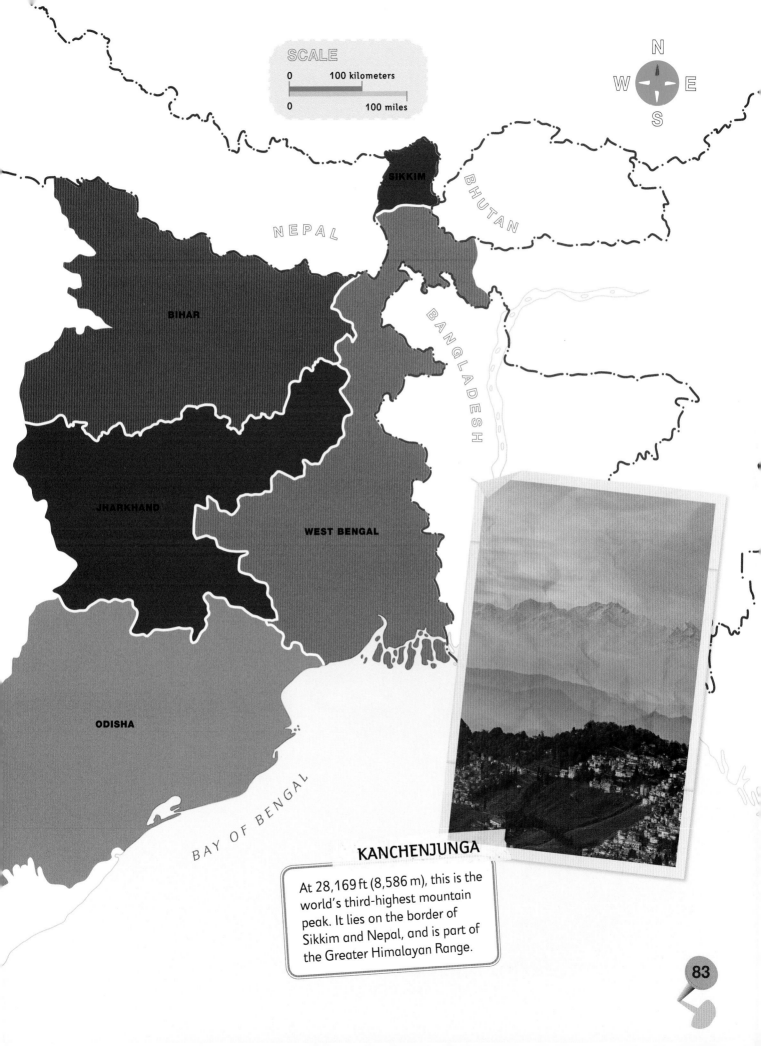

SCALE

0   100 kilometers

0   100 miles

N W E S

SIKKIM

NEPAL

BHUTAN

BANGLADESH

BIHAR

JHARKHAND

WEST BENGAL

ODISHA

BAY OF BENGAL

KANCHENJUNGA

At 28,169 ft (8,586 m), this is the world's third-highest mountain peak. It lies on the border of Sikkim and Nepal, and is part of the Greater Himalayan Range.

BIHAR

The state takes its name from the Sanskrit word for monastery. After all, it is the birthplace of Buddhism and the Jain *tirthankara*, Mahavira. The Mauryan empire and India's first centers of learning were also established here. Bihar lies in the fertile Gangetic Plains and agriculture is the mainstay for the majority of its people.

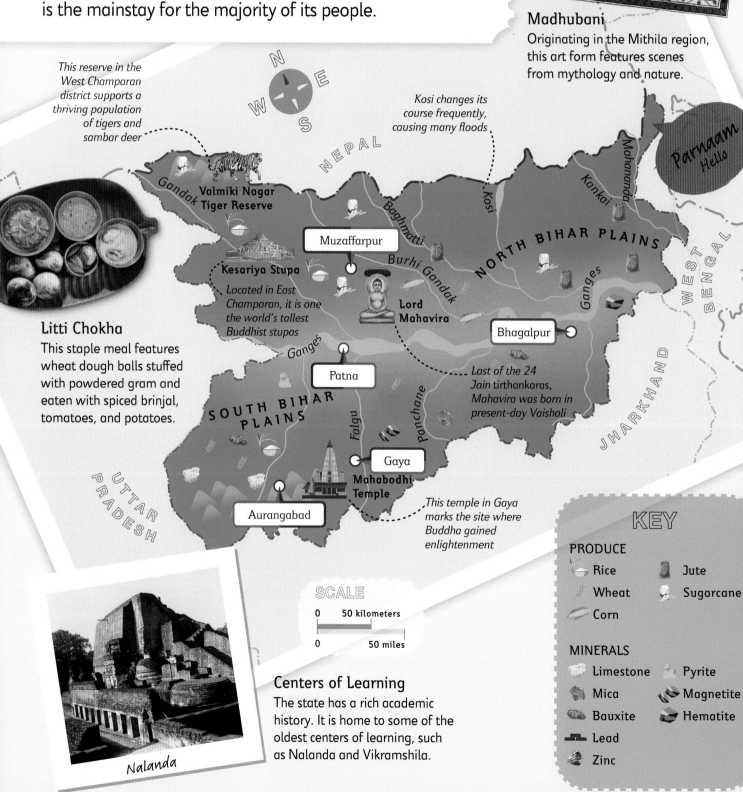

Madhubani
Originating in the Mithila region, this art form features scenes from mythology and nature.

This reserve in the West Champaran district supports a thriving population of tigers and sambar deer

Kosi changes its course frequently, causing many floods

Parnaam
Hello

Litti Chokha
This staple meal features wheat dough balls stuffed with powdered gram and eaten with spiced brinjal, tomatoes, and potatoes.

NEPAL

Gandak
Valmiki Nagar Tiger Reserve

Muzaffarpur

Baghmatti

Burhi Gandak

Kosi

Kankai

Mahananda

NORTH BIHAR PLAINS

Ganges

WEST BENGAL

Kesariya Stupa
Located in East Champaran, it is one the world's tallest Buddhist stupas

Lord Mahavira

Ganges

Patna

Bhagalpur

Last of the 24 Jain tirthankaras, Mahavira was born in present-day Vaishali

JHARKHAND

SOUTH BIHAR PLAINS

Falgu

Panchane

Gaya

Mahabodhi Temple

UTTAR PRADESH

Aurangabad

This temple in Gaya marks the site where Buddha gained enlightenment

Centers of Learning
The state has a rich academic history. It is home to some of the oldest centers of learning, such as Nalanda and Vikramshila.

Nalanda

SCALE

0   50 kilometers

0   50 miles

KEY

PRODUCE
- Rice
- Wheat
- Corn
- Jute
- Sugarcane

MINERALS
- Limestone
- Mica
- Bauxite
- Lead
- Zinc
- Pyrite
- Magnetite
- Hematite

Chhath

This four-day festival is dedicated to the sun god and his wife Usha. Devotees follow a strict routine of fasting, bathing, and offering prayers to the rising and setting sun.

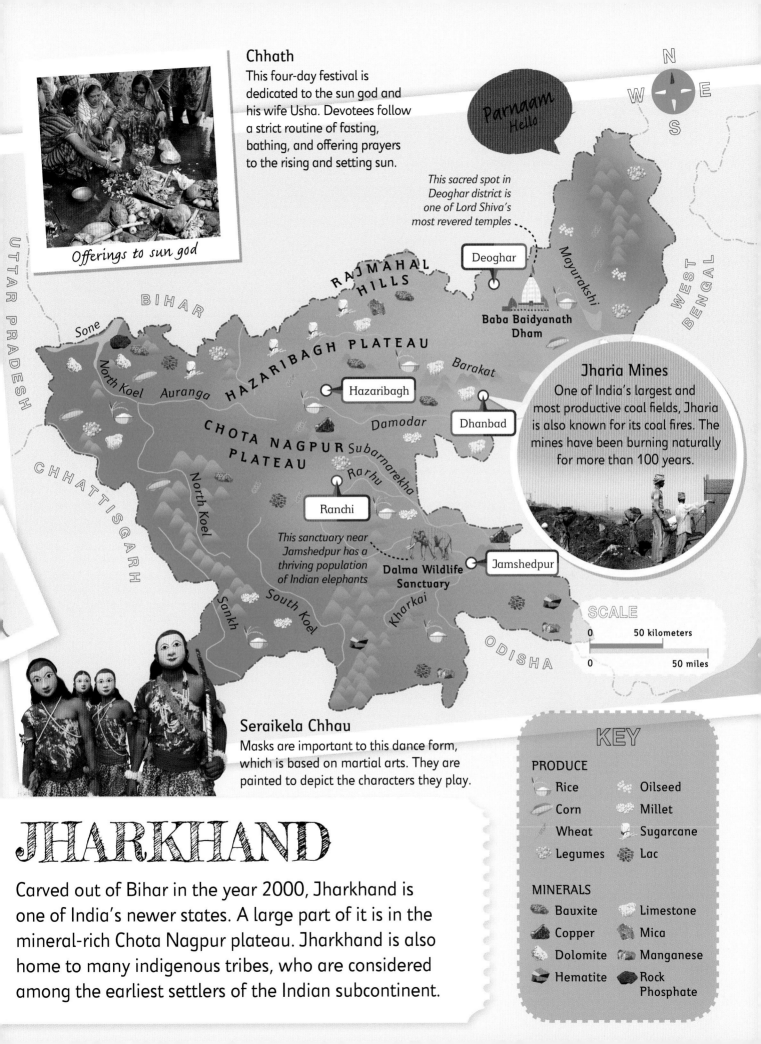

Offerings to sun god

Parnaam
Hello

This sacred spot in Deoghar district is one of Lord Shiva's most revered temples

Deoghar

Baba Baidyanath Dham

Jharia Mines

One of India's largest and most productive coal fields, Jharia is also known for its coal fires. The mines have been burning naturally for more than 100 years.

RAJMAHAL HILLS

BIHAR

Sone

Mayurakshi

WEST BENGAL

North Koel

Auranga

HAZARIBAGH PLATEAU

Barakat

Hazaribagh

Damodar

Dhanbad

UTTAR PRADESH

CHOTA NAGPUR PLATEAU

Subarnarekha

Rarhu

Ranchi

North Koel

CHHATTISGARH

This sanctuary near Jamshedpur has a thriving population of Indian elephants

Dalma Wildlife Sanctuary

Jamshedpur

Kharkai

South Koel

Sankh

ODISHA

SCALE

0 — 50 kilometers

0 — 50 miles

Seraikela Chhau

Masks are important to this dance form, which is based on martial arts. They are painted to depict the characters they play.

JHARKHAND

Carved out of Bihar in the year 2000, Jharkhand is one of India's newer states. A large part of it is in the mineral-rich Chota Nagpur plateau. Jharkhand is also home to many indigenous tribes, who are considered among the earliest settlers of the Indian subcontinent.

KEY

PRODUCE

- Rice
- Oilseed
- Corn
- Millet
- Wheat
- Sugarcane
- Legumes
- Lac

MINERALS

- Bauxite
- Limestone
- Copper
- Mica
- Dolomite
- Manganese
- Hematite
- Rock Phosphate

GREAT SITES

India's religious and cultural diversity and its long history of invaders have shaped the country's wealth of architectural marvels, from palaces and forts to memorials and places of worship.

MAN-MADE MARVEL

The state of Meghaylaya receives the most rainfall in the world. About 180 years ago, the Khasi tribes devised a solution to cross the swollen rivers of the state—living root bridges (p.74).

HERITAGE BUILDINGS

TAJ MAHAL, Uttar Pradesh

One of the seven wonders of the world and a fine example of Mughal architecture, this exquisite 17th-century mausoleum was built by emperor Shah Jahan in memory of his wife Mumtaz Mahal.

GROUP OF MONUMENTS AT HAMPI, Karnataka

This ancient capital city by the Tungabhadra river has many urban and religious structures including forts, temples, pillared halls, marketplaces, and shrines. They are considered a fine example of Dravidian architecture.

JANTAR MANTAR, Rajasthan

Built in the 18th century, this is the most elaborate of the five astronomical observatories constructed by Rajput ruler Sawai Jai Singh II. The site houses about 20 instruments called yantras.

PLACES OF WORSHIP

GREAT LIVING CHOLA TEMPLES, Tamil Nadu

The three grand complexes—the Brihadisvara temple in Thanjavur, and Gangaikonda Cholapuram, and Airavatesvara temple at Darasuram reflect the architectural prowess of the Chola dynasty.

SHORE TEMPLE, Tamil Nadu

Part of the group of monuments at Mamallapuram, also known as Mahabalipuram, this temple was built by the Pallava dynasty in the 8th century. It has been carved from a giant rock and has shrines of Shiva and Vishnu.

BARA IMAMBARA, Uttar Pradesh

Constructed in the late 18th century, this mosque was commissioned to provide employment to the people of the famine-struck city. It is believed that more than 20,000 men were employed for the construction of the complex.

DID YOU KNOW?

The oldest church in India, St. Thomas Syro-Malabar Catholic Church in Kerala, is believed to have been established around 52 CE by St. Thomas himself, one of the 12 apostles of Jesus Christ.

BHIMBETKA CAVES,
Madhya Pradesh

Indian archaeologist V.S. Wakankar discovered this site of about 700 rock shelters at Bhimbetka in 1957. A prime example of prehistoric art, many of these caves have paintings of wild animals.

TALATAL GHAR,
Assam

This sprawling complex in the Sivasagar district contains ruins of an army base built by the Ahom dynasty, who ruled present-day Assam for nearly 600 years.

UNAKOTI HERITAGE SITE,
Tripura

The Unakoti hills have giant bas-reliefs of Hindu gods and goddesses, especially Shiva and Ganesha, believed to date back to the 7th–8th century CE.

Dholavira
Built between two water channels, this 5,000-year-old town in Gujarat was dotted with reservoirs. Unlike the brick city of Mohenjodaro, Dholavira was mainly built from stone.

MYSURU PALACE,
Karnataka

The grandiose palace was designed by British architect Henry Irwin in the early 20th century. The three-story palace has ornate domes and sculpted pillars, and is surrounded by finely manicured gardens.

JAHAZ MAHAL,
Madhya Pradesh

This 15th-century palace is surrounded by two lakes and gives the impression of an anchored ship, especially during monsoon when the lakes are full. It is believed that the palace was staffed by about 15,000 women.

Lothal
Excavated on the banks of Bhogavo river in Gujarat, Lothal is the only port town of the Indus Valley Civilization. The remains reveal that the walls of the town were designed to resist the frequent flooding of the river.

KUMBHALGARH FORT,
Rajasthan

This massive 15th-century fort sits atop a tall hill offering a bird's-eye view of the region. Stretching for about 22 miles (36 km), the fort's walls are the second-longest in the world.

GWALIOR FORT,
Madhya Pradesh

This fort has come under the reign of many rulers. It was also the site where Tantia Tope and Lakshmi Bai fought against the British during the revolt of 1857.

SIKKIM

Bordering Bhutan, Nepal, and China, this mountainous state is nature's haven with craggy peaks, tranquil valleys, high passes, terraced tea gardens, and glacial lakes. Gangtok, the capital, is one of the cleanest cities in the country.

Thangka painting

A religious scroll usually made of cloth, *thangka* is a common sight at monasteries and Sikkimese houses. They typically depict the lives of gods and goddesses, with Buddha as the central figure.

Gurudongmar lake

At an altitude of about 17,800 ft (5,425 m), Gurudongmar is one of the highest lakes in the world. The freshwater lake is one of the sources of the Teesta, a river that runs across the length of the state.

Khangchendzonga National Park

A UNESCO World Heritage Site, this high-altitude park has a large number of flora and fauna species, including rare and endangered animals, such as the red panda, snow leopard, and musk deer.

Red panda

Kanchenjunga

Also known as Khangchendzonga, this mountain is an important part of the mythological and cultural rituals of the Sikkimese.

CHINA

Lachung

Lachung

Teesta

Teesta

Rangyong Chhu

GREATER HIMALAYAS

KANCHENJUNGA

N
W E
S

Kasto cha
How are you?

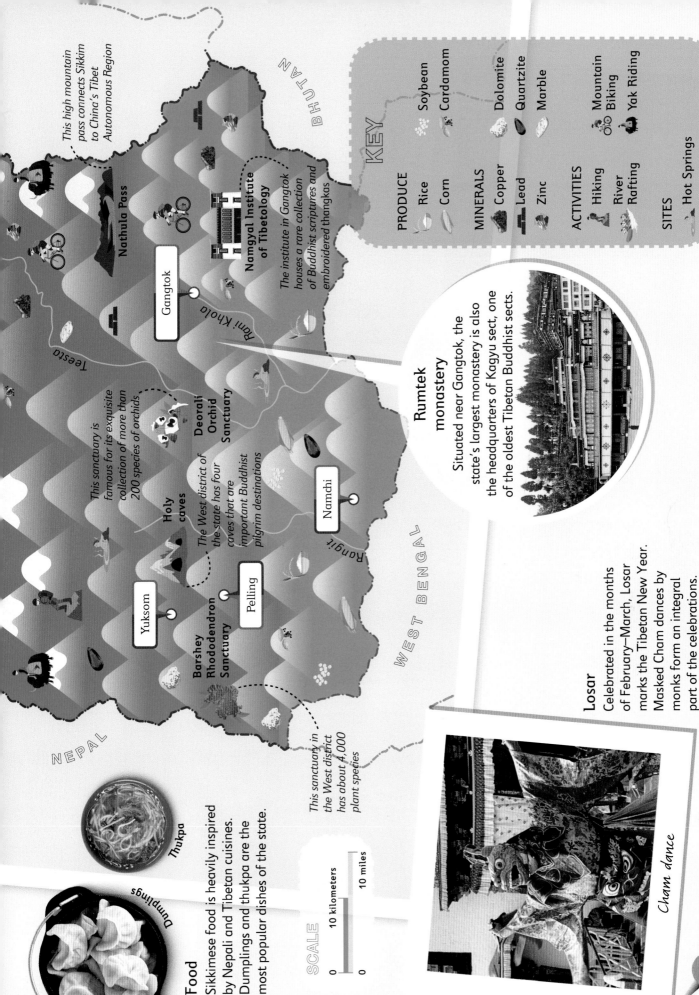

This high mountain pass connects Sikkim to China's Tibet Autonomous Region

Nathula Pass

Gangtok

Namgyal Institute of Tibetology
The institute in Gangtok houses a rare collection of Buddhist scriptures and embroidered thangkas

Teesta

Rani Khola

This sanctuary is famous for its exquisite collection of more than 200 species of orchids

Deorali Orchid Sanctuary

Holy caves

The West district of the state has four caves that are important Buddhist pilgrim destinations

Yuksom

Barshey Rhododendron Sanctuary

Pelling

Namchi

Rangit

This sanctuary in the West district has about 4,000 plant species

NEPAL

BHUTAN

WEST BENGAL

KEY

PRODUCE
Rice
Corn
Soybean
Cardamom

MINERALS
Copper
Lead
Zinc
Dolomite
Quartzite
Marble

ACTIVITIES
Hiking
River Rafting
Mountain Biking
Yak Riding

SITES
Hot Springs

Rumtek monastery
Situated near Gangtok, the state's largest monastery is also the headquarters of Kagyu sect, one of the oldest Tibetan Buddhist sects.

Losar
Celebrated in the months of February–March, Losar marks the Tibetan New Year. Masked Cham dances by monks form an integral part of the celebrations.

Cham dance

Food
Sikkimese food is heavily inspired by Nepali and Tibetan cuisines. Dumplings and thukpa are the most popular dishes of the state.

Thukpa

Dumplings

SCALE

0   10 kilometers

0   10 miles

WEST BENGAL

A hub of art and culture, this small, densely populated state has been the birthplace of great philosophers, painters, dancers, and singers. Its northern region is bound by the Himalayas and has the famous tea gardens of Darjeeling. The Sundarbans toward the south are part of the world's largest delta region.

Mangroves at Sundarbans

The Sundarbans

The largest mangrove forest in the world, the swampy lands of the Sundarbans are home to many endangered plants and animals, including the Bengal tiger.

The Indian rhinoceros is found in this national park situated in the Alipurduar district

BHUTAN

Also known as the Toy Train, it was started in 1881 and is now on the UNESCO World Heritage List

Jaldapara National Park

Darjeeling Himalayan Railroad

Darjeeling

Siliguri

NEPAL

Situated in the Malda district, these are the ruins of the largest mosque in the Indian subcontinent

Adina Mosque

BIHAR

SCALE

| 0 | 50 kilometers |
| 0 | 50 miles |

Rasgulla

This popular Bengali dessert, *rasgulla*, is made from soft balls of fresh paneer that are dipped in sugar syrup.

Nomoskar
Hello

N
E
W
S

Bauls

These wandering musicians from West Bengal and Bangladesh practice a form of devotional music. Their soulful music is believed to have inspired many, including Rabindranath Tagore.

Baul singers

Terra-cotta temples of Bishnupur

These 16th- and 17th-century temples are the remains of the Malla kingdom that ruled this region for 300 years. Many of these are dedicated to Krishna and Radha.

Durga Puja

One of West Bengal's most important festivals, Durga Puja celebrates the victory of Goddess Durga over the demon Mahishasura. Elaborate pandals are set up and many cultural activities are organized throughout the state.

Bankura horses

The terra-cotta horses from Bankura are made using a generations-old technique of molding clay. They are usually offered to deities as part of religious rituals.

BANGLADESH

Ganges

JHARKHAND

SUSUNIA HILLS

Murshidabad

This small town in Birbhum has a famous school set up by Tagore in 1901

Santiniketan

Asansol

Durgapur

Damodar

Hooghly

Rabindranath Tagore

Asia's first Nobel Laureate, Tagore, was born in Kolkata

Kolkata

Sundarbans

Raja Ram Mohan Roy

Born in 1772 in the present-day Hooghly district, this social reformer fought for women's rights

IIT, Kharagpur

The first Indian Institute of Technology opened in 1951

Kharagpur

ODISHA

BAY OF BENGAL

Kemon achhish? *How are you?*

KEY

PRODUCE
- Rice
- Wheat
- Corn
- Oilseeds
- Jute
- Tea
- Peanuts

MINERALS AND INDUSTRIES
- Coal
- China and Fire Clay
- Port

KOLKATA

Once known as Calcutta and central to the British Raj and the Indian freedom struggle, this city has transformed over the years. A prominent cultural hub today, all aspects of Kolkata evoke intense emotions—from the iconic Howrah Bridge to its noisy, crowded bazaars, and the notes of the conch shell during the *pujos*.

VICTORIA MEMORIAL

This symbolic landmark, opened to the public in 1921, was built in honor of Queen Victoria. It has one of the oldest museum libraries in India. Architect William Emerson envisioned the building as a mix of Egyptian, Venetian, Deccani, Mughal, and British styles.

IN HISTORY

Calcutta was made the capital of British India in 1772. This city remained the seat of power until 1911, when administrative roles were transferred to New Delhi.

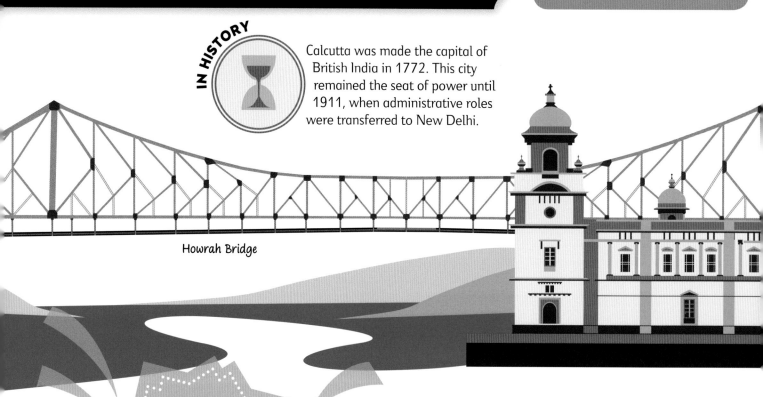

Howrah Bridge

WOW!

The Zoological Garden (Calcutta Zoo) is one of the oldest zoos in India.

80,000

The estimated seating capacity at Eden Gardens, India's largest and the world's third-largest cricket stadium.

TOP 5

1 The **tram** is the best way to explore the charming lanes of Kolkata. The Calcutta Tramways Company is India's only operating tram network.

2 Savor Kolkata's street food, from spicy **jhaal muris** and tangy **puchkas,** to the sweet and delicious **sondesh.**

3 Take a boat ride in the evening on the **Hooghly** and enjoy a view of the city's skyline, old and contemporary buildings, and an illuminated Howrah Bridge.

Statues of the demon-slaying Durga are sculpted at the potters' village of Kumartuli. Dating back some 300 years, this quarter is home to families who work and live here. The artisans spend the entire year sculpting intricately detailed idols just in time for Durga Puja.

POPULAR CULTURE IN INDIA

From love stories, such as Sarat Chandra Chattopadhyay's *Parineeta*, to the tales of detective Byomkesh Bakshi, Kolkata has been the muse for many writers.

FAMOUS FACES

The city has given birth to great gems, such as Nobel laureate Rabindranath Tagore, filmmaker Satyajit Ray, and mathematician and physicist S.N. Bose.

MAD ABOUT

Soccer and the bakery Flurys

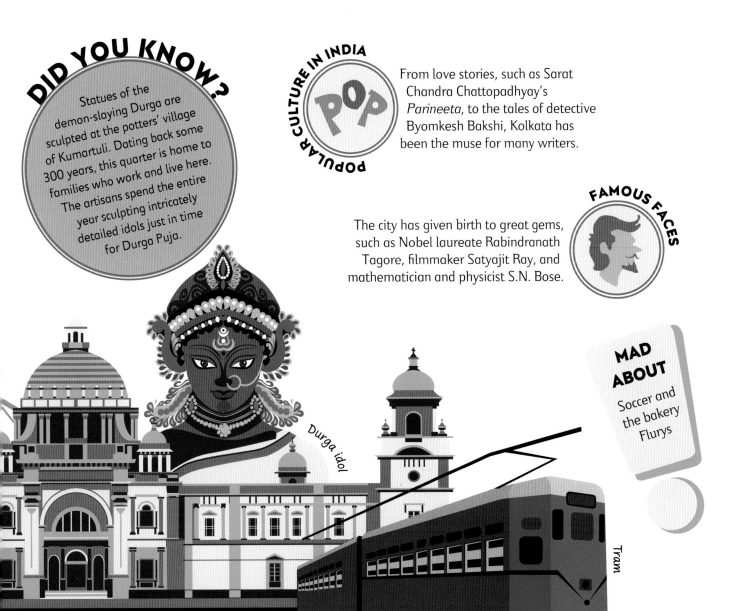

Durga idol

Tram

Victoria Memorial

The Acharya Jagadish Chandra Bose Indian Botanical Garden is home to one of the widest trees in the world—the Great Banyan. It is more than 250 years old and is spread across four acres.

GREEN POCKET

"Let Calcutta suffuse your being, invade your bloodstream, and steal your soul. But once you have, you'll love Calcutta forever."

Vir Sanghvi, Journalist

4 During Durga Puja, go **pandal hopping**. Each pandal is unique—some are traditional, while others are made of glass, or at times even designed to look like a musical concert stage or circus tent.

5 Drive over the iconic **Howrah Bridge**. Inaugurated in 1943, it was the third-longest cantilever bridge in the world at the time. This unique bridge style has supports only on one side!

ODISHA

Enveloped by the forested hills of the Eastern Ghats and the coastline of Bay of Bengal, this state is a treasure trove of natural and architectural marvels. Odisha is blessed with a rich cultural heritage with numerous historical and religious monuments.

It is the longest dam in the world ·····

Hirakud Dam

Pattachitra painting

Traditional cloth painting

Although Lord Jagannath is the most popular subject of the cloth painting tradition Pattachitra, it can also feature stories from Hindu epics and myths.

Nomokoro mela

This dance form developed in the temples as an offering to the deities ·····

SCALE

0   50 kilometers

0   50 miles

Sun Temple, Konark

This 13th-century temple is designed in the shape of the chariot that carries the sun god on his journey across the sky. The 24 wheels represent the number of hours in a day and the seven horses are the seven days of the week.

Odissi

The holy Banyan is Odisha's state tree ·····

Banyan tree

CHHATTISGARH

EASTERN GHATS

ANDHRA PRADESH

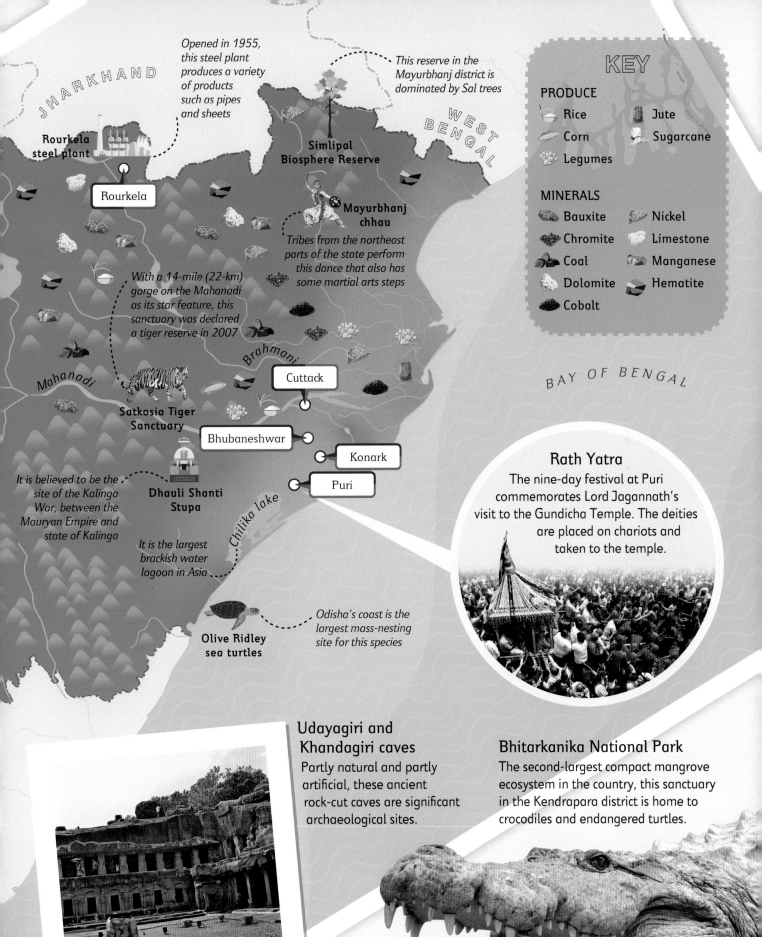

JHARKHAND

Opened in 1955, this steel plant produces a variety of products such as pipes and sheets

Rourkela steel plant

Rourkela

This reserve in the Mayurbhanj district is dominated by Sal trees

WEST BENGAL

Simlipal Biosphere Reserve

Mayurbhanj chhau

Tribes from the northeast parts of the state perform this dance that also has some martial arts steps

With a 14-mile (22-km) gorge on the Mahanadi as its star feature, this sanctuary was declared a tiger reserve in 2007

Mahanadi

Brahmani

Cuttack

Satkosia Tiger Sanctuary

Bhubaneshwar

Konark

Puri

It is believed to be the site of the Kalinga War, between the Mauryan Empire and state of Kalinga

Dhauli Shanti Stupa

Chilika lake

It is the largest brackish water lagoon in Asia

Olive Ridley sea turtles

Odisha's coast is the largest mass-nesting site for this species

BAY OF BENGAL

KEY

PRODUCE
- Rice
- Jute
- Corn
- Sugarcane
- Legumes

MINERALS
- Bauxite
- Nickel
- Chromite
- Limestone
- Coal
- Manganese
- Dolomite
- Hematite
- Cobalt

Rath Yatra

The nine-day festival at Puri commemorates Lord Jagannath's visit to the Gundicha Temple. The deities are placed on chariots and taken to the temple.

Udayagiri and Khandagiri caves

Partly natural and partly artificial, these ancient rock-cut caves are significant archaeological sites.

Bhitarkanika National Park

The second-largest compact mangrove ecosystem in the country, this sanctuary in the Kendrapara district is home to crocodiles and endangered turtles.

Khandagiri caves

The city of Hampi has more than 1,600 monuments, including forts, temples, and shrines. (p.101)

Farmers anoint their plows with sandalwood paste before harvesting rice, as part of Thai Pongal festivities. (p.111)

The 58 ft-(17-m)high Gomateshwara statue is anointed with milk and saffron, from head to toe, once every 12 years. (p.101)

Chinese explorer Zheng He introduced Chinese fishing nets to the fishermen of Kochi. (p.121)

SOUTH INDIA

The southern states of India have been shaped over 2,000 years by the rise and fall of dynasties including the Cholas, Pandyas, and Chalukyas, each having left their mark on the region's sociocultural landscape. With its many mangroves and lagoons, the area is also a haven for biodiversity.

Surrounded by the Arabian Sea on one side and the Bay of Bengal on the other, the vast coastline of the region is not only picturesque, but also a major contributor to the trade of fisheries.

COASTLINE

SCALE

0   150 kilometers

0   150 miles

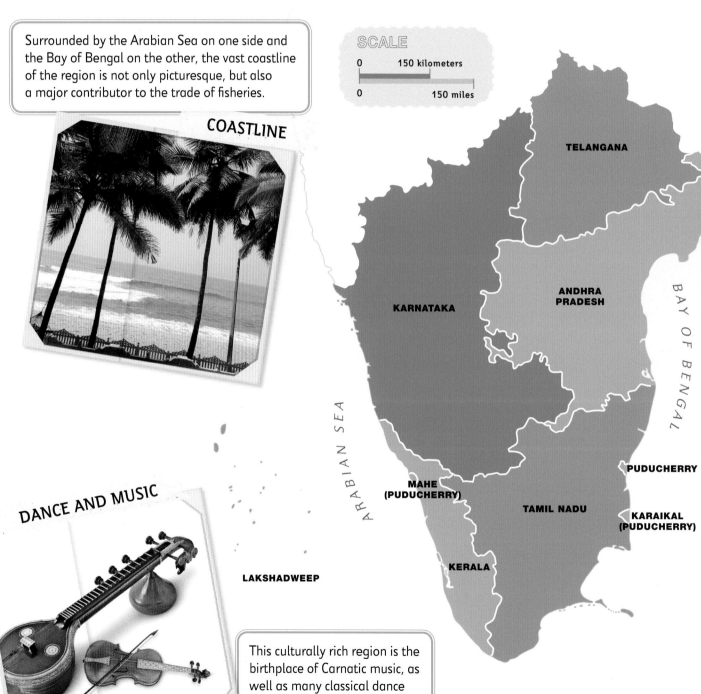

TELANGANA

KARNATAKA

ANDHRA PRADESH

BAY OF BENGAL

ARABIAN SEA

MAHE (PUDUCHERRY)

PUDUCHERRY

TAMIL NADU

KARAIKAL (PUDUCHERRY)

KERALA

LAKSHADWEEP

DANCE AND MUSIC

This culturally rich region is the birthplace of Carnatic music, as well as many classical dance forms, such as Bharatanatyam, Mohiniyattam, and Kathakali.

NILGIRI HILLS

The picturesque Nilgiri hills lie at the junction of the Eastern and Western Ghats. They are covered in grasslands and evergreen forests and are home to many tribal groups, including the pastoral community Todas. The region is known for its tea and coffee plantations.

YANAM (PUDUCHERRY)

N
W • E
S

ANDAMAN AND NICOBAR ISLANDS

BOAT RACES

The snake boats of Kerala that were once used to ferry warriors are now lavishly decorated to participate in thrilling races called Vallamkali. The Nehru Trophy Boat Race, introduced in 1952, is the most famous of these.

TEMPLE ARCHITECTURE

The temples of Tamil Nadu, built from the 7th to the 18th century, employ the Dravidian style of architecture. Enclosed within a compound wall, the temples are characterized by pyramidal towers, entrance gateways called gopuras, and pillared halls called mandapams. The Brihadisvara and Ranganathaswamy temples are important examples of the style.

Brihadisvara Temple, Tamil Nadu

KARNATAKA

From the forested slopes of the Western Ghats, to the comparatively dry landscape near the Deccan Plateau, Karnataka has diverse terrain. Its ancient temples, magnificent palaces, and medieval forts reflect its rich history. The state is a leading producer of coffee, spices, and fruits.

Sericulture
Famous for its handloom industry, Karnataka is also the country's largest producer of silk. Different regions in the state have their own distinct styles, with Mysore silk being one of the most popular. It is traditionally woven using gold threads.

Mysore silk

KEY

PRODUCE
- Rice
- Corn
- Ragi
- Cotton
- Sugarcane
- Coffee
- Betel nut

MINERALS AND INDUSTRIES
- Bauxite
- Chromite
- Gold
- Hematite
- Manganese
- Sericulture
- Mangnetite

SITES
- Tiger Reserve

MAHARASHTRA

TELENGANA

ANDHRA PRADESH

Manjira

Krishna

Bhima

Bidriware

Bidar

This intricate metal handicraft was brought to India from Iran

Gol Gumbaz

Bijapur

The dome of Muhammad Adil Shah's mausoleum at Vijayapura is one of the largest domes in India

BADAMI HILLS

Badami caves

This set of four cave temples at Badami was built about 1,500 years ago by the Chalukyas

Badami

Pattadakal

A UNESCO World Heritage Site in the Bagalkot district, it has about 150 Hindu and Jain temples

Belagavi

Hubballi

SCALE
```
0        50 kilometers
0        50 miles
```

Hampi
Once the capital of the Vijayanagara Empire, Hampi has many intricately carved temples, palaces, pavilions, and market spaces, which tell of a glorious past.

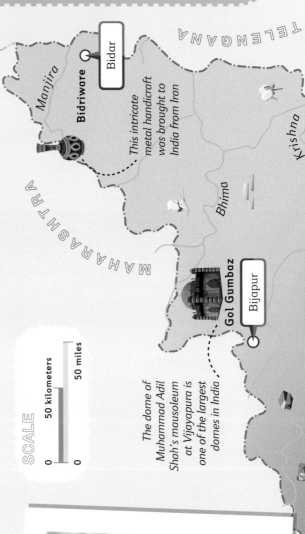

Vijaya Vittala Temple at Hampi

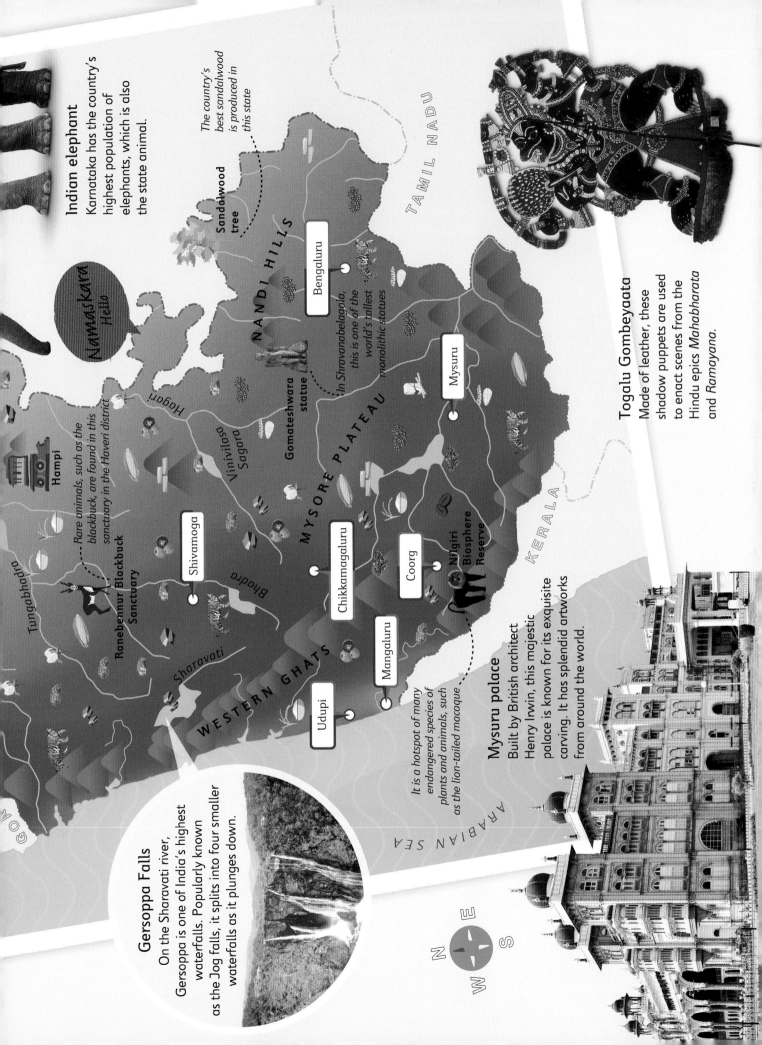

Indian elephant
Karnataka has the country's highest population of elephants, which is also the state animal.

The country's best sandalwood is produced in this state

Sandalwood tree

NANDI HILLS

TAMIL NADU

Bengaluru

In Shravanabelagola, this is one of the world's tallest monolithic statues

Gomateshwara statue

Mysuru

Togalu Gombeyaata
Made of leather, these shadow puppets are used to enact scenes from the Hindu epics *Mahabharata* and *Ramayana*.

Namaskara
Hello

Hogan

Vinivilasa Sagara

MYSORE PLATEAU

Rare animals, such as the blackbuck, are found in this sanctuary in the Haveri district

Hampi

Tungabhadra

Ranebennur Blackbuck Sanctuary

Shivamoga

Bhadra

Chikkamagaluru

Coorg

Nilgiri Biosphere Reserve

KERALA

Sharavati

WESTERN GHATS

Mangaluru

Udupi

It is a hotspot of many endangered species of plants and animals, such as the lion-tailed macaque

Mysuru palace
Built by British architect Henry Irwin, this majestic palace is known for its exquisite carving. It has splendid artworks from around the world.

ARABIAN SEA

GOA

Gersoppa Falls
On the Sharavati river, Gersoppa is one of India's highest waterfalls. Popularly known as the Jog falls, it splits into four smaller waterfalls as it plunges down.

N
W E
S

BENGALURU

The capital of Karnataka is a city where the old and new exist side-by-side. A tolerant climate, stunning, palatial, green gardens, medieval fortresses, and ruins are juxtaposed with the city's cosmopolitan air, fast-paced lifestyle, and a constantly evolving tech world.

Tech parks

IN HISTORY

The city gets its name from *bendakaluru*, or boiled beans, the meal 12th-century Hoysala king Veera Ballala II was offered by an elderly lady when he lost his way. Grateful, the king remembered the area as "Bendakaluru," which turned to Bengaluru over the course of time.

Kempe Gowda

177
The number of acres covered by the lush and green Cubbon Park.

WOW!
Bengaluru is the first city in Asia to get streetlights. In 1905, about 100 electrical lights replaced kerosene lamps in many areas in the city.

TOP 5

1 For a panoramic view of the city, take a boat ride on **Ulsoor Lake.** A paved path around the lake offers a stunning view of high-rise glass skyscrapers.

2 The **Bangalore Palace** was built in 1887 by the Wodeyar dynasty. The palace, inspired by Tudor-style architecture, has a lot of art from the bygone era.

3 **Nandi Hills,** or Nandidurga, is an ancient hill fortress about 40 miles (60 km) away from the city. Locals drive up early to catch a glimpse of the scenic sunrise above the clouds.

VIDHANA SOUDHA

Sprawled across 60 acres, this iconic structure was built to commemorate Bengaluru's position as the administrative capital of unified Karnataka in 1956. The building is known for its blend of ancient and modern architectural styles. It appears even more regal and grand on Sunday evenings when it is illuminated with many colorful lights.

DID YOU KNOW?

Bengaluru is home to a rock hill made of 3,000 million-years-old peninsular gneiss. This metamorphic rock formation can be found in Lalbagh Botanical Gardens and is unique to the southern peninsular region.

GREEN POCKET

The city is studded with fragrant and colorful trees. These include purple jacarandas, pink poui, yellow cassia blossoms, and white jasmine, along with another 140,000 varieties. This is possibly why Bengaluru is known as the Garden City of India.

Vidhana Soudha

MAD ABOUT

Filter coffee

Nandi temple

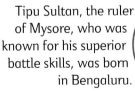

Tipu Sultan, the ruler of Mysore, who was known for his superior battle skills, was born in Bengaluru.

FAMOUS FACES

Bengaluru is the backdrop to many iconic films such as *Coolie* (1983), *Mard* (1985), and *Ghayal* (1985). The blockbuster, *Sholay* (1975) was also shot close to the city.

POPULAR CULTURE IN INDIA
POP

4 Built by Kempe Gowda, a legendary ruler, the **Bull Temple** has a stone monolith of Shiva's bull Nandi, about 20 ft (6 m) tall. Legend says it keeps getting taller!

5 **Tipu Sultan's Summer Palace** was first constructed in 1537 and used to be the mud fort of Kempe Gowda. It was later renovated by Tipu Sultan and his father Hyder Ali, the subsequent rulers of the city.

TELANGANA

India's youngest state, Telangana was formed in 2014. Most of its land is a part of the Deccan Plateau, covered in red soil and dotted with isolated hills. The state lies at the intersection of northern and southern India, and is considered the meeting point of different cultures.

SCALE

0   50 kilometers

0   50 miles

Warangal Fort

Warangal

The city was the ancient capital of the Kakatiya dynasty. The rulers were renowned for their architectural and engineering genius. The Warangal Fort is a prime example.

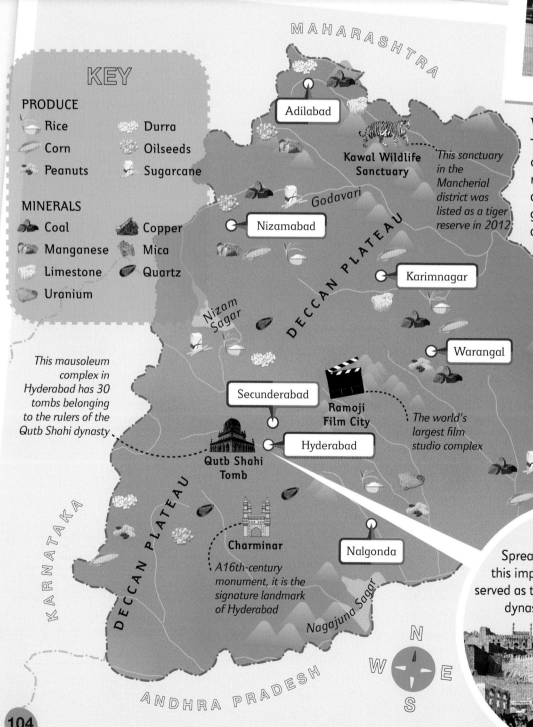

KEY

PRODUCE
- Rice
- Corn
- Peanuts
- Durra
- Oilseeds
- Sugarcane

MINERALS
- Coal
- Manganese
- Limestone
- Uranium
- Copper
- Mica
- Quartz

MAHARASHTRA

Adilabad

Kawal Wildlife Sanctuary

This sanctuary in the Mancherial district was listed as a tiger reserve in 2012

Godavari

Nizamabad

DECCAN PLATEAU

Karimnagar

Nizam Sagar

Warangal

CHHATTISGARH

Vandanalu Hello

This mausoleum complex in Hyderabad has 30 tombs belonging to the rulers of the Qutb Shahi dynasty

Secunderabad

Ramoji Film City

The world's largest film studio complex

Hyderabad

Khammam

Qutb Shahi Tomb

KARNATAKA

DECCAN PLATEAU

Charminar

A 16th-century monument, it is the signature landmark of Hyderabad

Nalgonda

Nagajuna Sagar

N
W   E
S

ANDHRA PRADESH

Golconda Fort

Spread across 3 miles (5 km), this impressive fort in Hyderabad served as the capital of the Qutb Shahi dynasty in the 16th century.

ANDHRA PRADESH

The terrain of this state ranges from the scenic beaches of Visakhapatnam along the Coromandel Coast to the famous paddy fields of Nellore, which give the state its nickname—the rice bowl of India. Andhra Pradesh is also known for its vibrant art and craft that speaks volumes of its rich cultural heritage.

This dance gets its name from the place of its origin, Kuchipudi village

Vandanalu Hello

Kuchipudi

Lights at Borra

Borra caves
Lined with limestone, these magnificent caves were discovered in 1807 by the Geological Survey of India. They are considered one of the deepest caves in the country.

It is the second-longest river of India

It is the largest tiger reserve in the country

Visakhapatnam

Godavari

Nagarjunsagar Srisailam Tiger Reserve

Vijayawada

Amravati

While Amravati is the de facto capital, Hyderabad is the de jure capital of the state

KARNATAKA

DECCAN PLATEAU

TELENGANA

CHHATTISGARH

ODISHA

EASTERN GHATS

BAY OF BENGAL

Kurnool

More than 50,000 pilgrims visit this Hindu temple in Tirupati every day

Tirupati

Venkateswara Temple

TAMIL NADU

Bright colors of kalamkari

Kalamkari
This art of painting cotton fabric uses a *kalam*, or pen, to depict mythological characters, as well as flora and fauna.

Kondapalli toys
These lightweight wooden toys are famous for their intricate carving and bright colors. Small pieces of wood are first carved and then stuck together using an adhesive made of crushed tamarind seeds.

KEY

PRODUCE

Rice	Sugarcane
Corn	Peanuts
Cotton	

MINERALS AND INDUSTRIES

Baryte	Hematite
Diamond	Iron
Mica	Magnetite
Garnet	Manganese
Limestone	Oil and Natural Gas
Coal	

SCALE

0 —— 100 kilometers

0 —— 100 miles

HYDERABAD

This city was once confined as a grid along the Charminar and the banks of the Musi river. Once India's biggest and richest princely state, today Hyderabad is a burgeoning high-tech city that's still reminiscent of the opulence of the old days.

IN HISTORY

During the British Raj, Hyderabad was the only major princely state to have its own currency. Its Halli *sicca*, or Osmania *sicca* rupee, was used until 1959.

DID YOU KNOW?

Legend has it that the city was initially named Bhagyanagar after Bhagmati, Muhammad Quli Qutb Shah's wife. It is said that she later changed her name to Hyder Mahal and the city was renamed in her honor.

CHARMINAR

Muhammad Quli Qutb Shah, founder of the city, commissioned this monument in 1591 to celebrate the end of a plague. A highlight of the Qutb Shahi dynasty, this 216-ft (66-m) high, four-column structure is an impressive sight. In fact, the old city of Hyderabad was designed with the monument as the center. The surrounding area was a hub of business.

Charminar

Buddha statue of Hyderabad

Golconda Fort

POPULAR CULTURE IN INDIA

POP

The novel *White Mughals* (2002) by William Dalrymple is a love story of a British man and a Mughal princess set in 19th-century Hyderabad.

TOP 5

1 Within the heart-shaped **Hussain Sagar Lake** is the 60-ft (18-m) high Buddha Statue of Hyderabad, one of the world's tallest monoliths of Gautama Buddha.

2 Visit **Ramoji Film City,** the world's largest film studio complex, according to the Guinness World Records. Its attractions include a theme park, bird parks, a studio tour, and live shows.

> "See how the speckled sky burns like a pigeon's throat,
> Jeweled with embers of opal and peridot."
> Sarojini Naidu, "Nightfall In the City Of Hyderabad"

WOW!
Hyderabad is the chief producer of natural pearls, which is how it got the name City of Pearls.

GREEN POCKET

Covering an area of about 350 acres, the Kasu Brahmananda Reddy National Park is the city's largest green space, with more than 600 plant species, including five insect-eating plants.

The third President of India, Zakir Hussain, and freedom fighter and political activist Sarojini Naidu are both from Hyderabad.

FAMOUS FACES

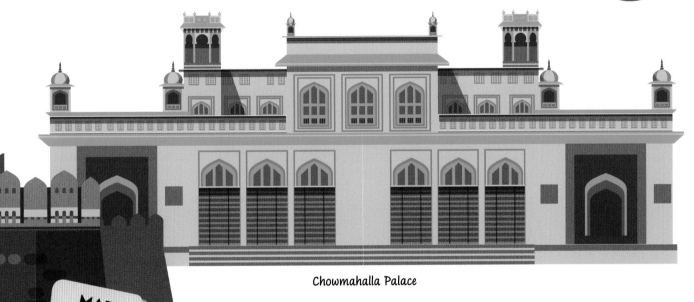

Chowmahalla Palace

MAD ABOUT
Hyderabadi biryani

7.2MILES
The length of the PVNR Expressway, India's longest flyover. Named after former Primer Minister P.V. Narasimha Rao, this elevated freeway connects the city to its international airport.

3 The **Salar Jung Museum** has artifacts, paintings, and manuscripts from all over the world curated by Salar Jung III, a prime minister of the former princely state of Hyderabad.

4 For a flavor of the old city, visit **Golconda Fort**, capital of the Qutb Shahi dynasty. Explore the ruins of palaces, mosques, and a 436-ft (130-m) high pavillion.

5 The luxurious **Chowmahalla Palace** was built in the 19th century. It was a ceremonial darbar and the residence of many Nizams.

RELIGIONS & FESTIVALS

India is the birthplace of four major religions of the world. The country has also welcomed people of all belief systems. This kaleidoscope of faiths has contributed to a colorful and culturally diverse annual holiday calendar.

DID YOU KNOW?

About 25 percent of the world's population follows the four religions that were founded in India—Hinduism, Buddhism, Jainism, and Sikhism.

RELIGIONS

HINDUISM

Believed to date back to 1500 BCE, Hinduism is a combination of many practices and texts such as the Vedas and the Upanishads. Other than India, Hinduism is prevalent in many Southeast Asian countries.

ISLAM

Islam was established in India through the first Delhi sultans who came from Afghanistan around 1200 CE. The religion was later integrated into India's culture during the Mughal empire. Today, it's the second-largest religion in the country.

CHRISTIANITY

The first evidence of Christianity in India comes from 52–54 CE when St. Thomas the Apostle came to India to spread the gospel of Christ. The expansion of the religion was attributed to the Catholic and Protestant missionaries in the 16th century .

FESTIVALS

Dussehra
This Hindu festival celebrates the triumph of good over evil.

Eid al-Fitr
This Muslim festival marks the end of Ramadan, a month-long period of strict fasting from dawn to dusk.

Holi
The festival of colors ushers in spring and is celebrated throughout north India.

Diwali
Known as the festival of lights, it signifies the victory of light over darkness.

Guru Nanak Jayanti
The birth of Guru Nanak, the first Sikh Guru, is celebrated with the lighting of candles.

Baisakhi
This Sikh harvest festival takes place after the rabi crop is ready for harvesting.

SIKHISM

This religion was founded by Guru Nanak, a poet and philosopher in 15th century CE. The followers, who are known as Sikhs, worship the holy book Granth Sahib and believe that God is one.

JAINISM

Jainism was given its present-day form by Mahavir. The followers, known as Jains, believe in nonviolence and respect all life forms.

BUDDHISM

Buddhism was founded between the 4th and 6th century BCE by Siddhartha Gautama (or Buddha), a prince who renounced everything to embark on a quest seeking enlightenment. Buddhism is based on the idea that nothing in the world is permanent.

BAHA'ISM

The Baha'i faith is one of the youngest religions in the world. It was founded by Mirza Husayn Ali, also known as Bahá'u'lláh, in Persia. It came to India shortly after it was founded in 1853 CE. Baha'i followers believe in the unity of all religions and people.

ZOROASTRIANISM

With its origins in modern-day Iran, this faith dates back to the 6th–7th century BCE. A priest named Zarathustra laid the tenets of the religion. The followers, in India, are known as Parsis who believe in one god and in the eternal battle between good and evil.

JUDAISM

It is a monotheistic religion like Islam and Christianity. Of the seven Jewish communities in India, the oldest resides in Cochin. They are said to be descendants of the traders of Judea, who came to Kerala in 562 BCE.

Christmas
Celebrated on December 25, it commemorates the birth of Jesus Christ.

Buddha Purnima
The birth of Gautama Buddha is celebrated on a full moon night in spring by lighting candles and exchanging gifts.

Navroz Festival
The Parsi New Year also marks the first day of spring.

Easter
This Christian festival celebrates the resurrection of Jesus Christ.

Mahavir Jayanti
A principal Jain religious day, it marks the birth of Mahavir, the last Tirthankara, or great teacher.

Eid al-Adha
This festival marks the completion of the annual Hajj pilgrimage.

TAMIL NADU

This state extends from the Coromandel Coast in the east to the forested Western Ghats in the west. Many towns in Tamil Nadu have the prefix "tiru," which means sacred and indicates the presence of a major religious site. This culturally rich state is also the land of Bharatanatyam, Kanjivaram silk, and Thanjavur paintings.

Chola bronzes

The Chola rulers, who came to power in the 9th century, were great patrons of art, music, and dance. They are best known for the bronze sculptures of deities made during their reign. Beeswax, sand, and clay was used to mold these intricately detailed statues.

Vanakkam
Hello

Palmyra is recognized as the official tree of the state

Palmyra tree

India's longest beach is in Chennai

Chennai

Marina Beach

The Tamil film industry produces some of the highest-grossing films in India

Tamil film industry

Geologists have found many fossilized dinosaur eggs in the state that are about 65 million years old

Dinosaur eggs

A heavy, bowlike structure, Kavadi is an offering to Lord Murugan, the god of war

Kavadi Attam

ANDHRA PRADESH

NAGARI HILLS

Palar

Cheyyar

JAVADI HILLS

Ponniyar

MELAGIRI HILLS

SHEVAROY HILLS

Kaveri

Kaveri

Bhavanisagar Reservoir

Noyyal

Moyar

KARNATAKA

NILGIRI HILLS

Salem

Thanjavur

Ooty

Coimbatore

N E W S

Textiles

The textile industry is a major source of employment for the state. The classic Kanjivaram silk, often woven with gold thread, is the state's most famous textile.

Kanjivaram silk

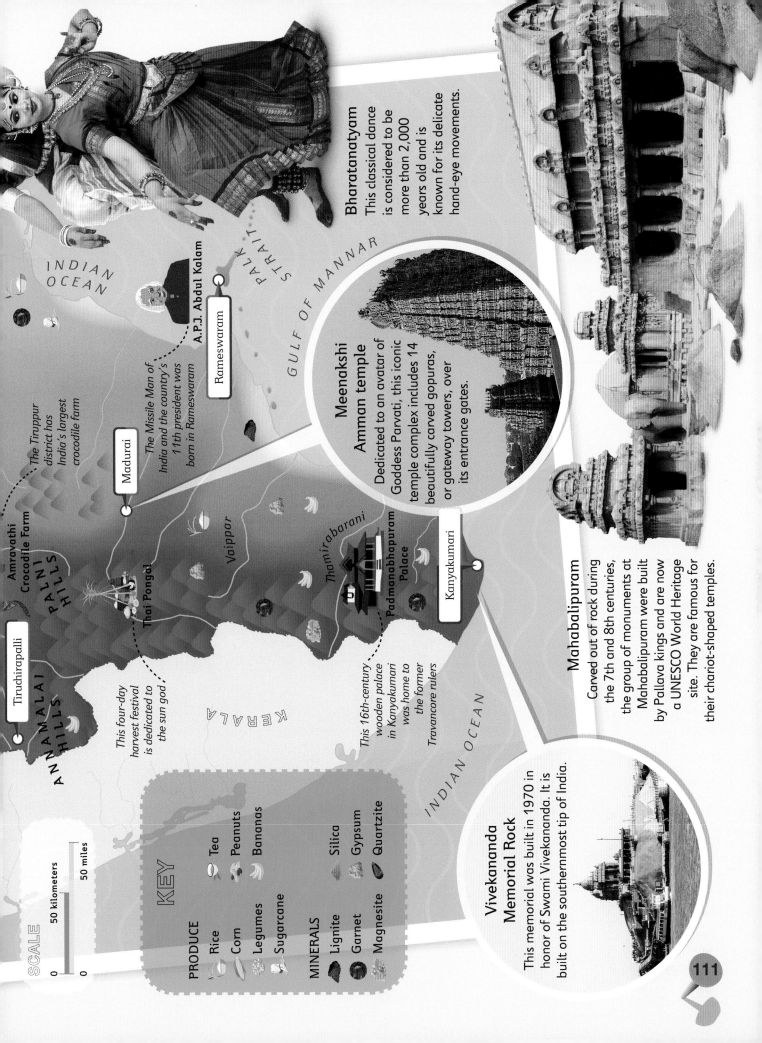

Bharatanatyam
This classical dance is considered to be more than 2,000 years old and is known for its delicate hand-eye movements.

INDIAN OCEAN

PALK STRAIT

GULF OF MANNAR

A.P.J. Abdul Kalam

Rameswaram

The Missile Man of India and the country's 11th president was born in Rameswaram

Madurai

Tiruchirapalli

The Tiruppur district has India's largest crocodile farm

Amravathi Crocodile Farm

PALNI HILLS

Thai Pongal

This four-day harvest festival is dedicated to the sun god

ANNAMALAI HILLS

KERALA

Vaippar

Thamirabarani

Padmanabhapuram Palace

This 16th-century wooden palace in Kanyakumari was home to the former Travancore rulers

Kanyakumari

INDIAN OCEAN

Meenakshi Amman temple
Dedicated to an avatar of Goddess Parvati, this iconic temple complex includes 14 beautifully carved gopuras, or gateway towers, over its entrance gates.

Mahabalipuram
Carved out of rock during the 7th and 8th centuries, the group of monuments at Mahabalipuram were built by Pallava kings and are now a UNESCO World Heritage site. They are famous for their chariot-shaped temples.

Vivekananda Memorial Rock
This memorial was built in 1970 in honor of Swami Vivekananda. It is built on the southernmost tip of India.

SCALE
0   50 kilometers
0   50 miles

KEY

PRODUCE
Rice
Corn
Legumes
Sugarcane
Tea
Peanuts
Bananas

MINERALS
Lignite
Garnet
Magnesite
Silica
Gypsum
Quartzite

CHENNAI

Once a cluster of fishing villages, Chennai, or Madras as it used to be known, is today called the gateway to South India. Many things about this city spark a sense of warmth, from its palm trees, salty sea air, and the scent of jasmine to memories of its rich cultural past.

DID YOU KNOW?

Chennai was the only Indian city that was fired on during WWI. On September 22, 1914, the German cruise ship *SMS Emden* allegedly reached the Bay of Bengal close to the coast of Madras. After identifying some British oil tankers, they reportedly fired, destroying more than 300,000 gallons of fuel, and then retreated.

WOW!

Established in 1688, the city's municipal corporation is one of the country's oldest.

MAD ABOUT

M.G. Ramachandran and Rajinikanth

Santhome Basilica

M.G. Ramachandran

Valluvar Kottam

Pallikaranai wetlands

TOP 5

1 The **Parthasarathy Temple** is a result of the work of three dynasties—the Pallavas, Cholas, and the Vijayanagara empire. This pyramid structure with elaborate carvings is one of the oldest temples in Chennai.

2 Built in the 16th century by the Portuguese, the **Santhome Basilica** is the home of the remains of St. Thomas the Apostle. He is believed to have come to India in about 52 CE to spread the message of Christianity.

Madras is short for Madraspatnam, a fishing village that was turned into a British trading post in 1639. By the 1800s, the British had made this city their commercial capital. Many years later in 1996, its name changed to Chennai.

"A city of dualities—conservative in its fashions, modern in its industry, schizophrenic in its romances. A stronghold for music, dance, mathematics, chess."

Tishani Doshi, writer

The Pallikaranai wetlands is the largest marshy region in Tamil Nadu. Many resident and migratory birds, from flamingoes, swamp hens, and sandpipers, to the common coots, are found here.

KAPALEESWARAR TEMPLE

Known for its vibrant rainbow colors, this temple was built in typical Dravidian architectural style in devotion to an avatar of Lord Shiva. The temple towers (*gopuras*) and pillars (*mandapams*) are decorated with his vehicles (or *vahanas*) including the bull, elephant, bandicoot rat, peacock, goat, and parrot.

Chennai is home to many accomplished personalities including author R.K. Narayan and chess grandmaster Viswanathan Anand.

8 MILES

The length of Marina Beach, the longest urban beach in India.

Kapaleeshwarar Temple

Food traditionally served on a banana leaf

POP

The Dev Patel film *The Man Who Knew Infinity* (2016) and Mani Ratnam's *Aaytha Ezhuthu* (2004) were both shot in the city's prestigious Presidency College.

3 The second largest in India, the **Government Museum** has 6 buildings and 46 galleries. It's known for its coin and bronze collections.

4 **Fort St. George** was built in 1644, when the city was relatively uninhabited. This British fortress houses the oldest Anglican church in India.

5 The monument **Valluvar Kottam**, commissioned in honor of Tamil poet Thiruvalluvar, displays his work inscribed on sculptures.

ANDAMAN AND NICOBAR ISLANDS

The archipelago of 572 islands in the Bay of Bengal is actually a submerged mountain range extending from Myanmar to Indonesia. Its tropical forests, mangroves, and coral reefs are home to a remarkable variety of flora and fauna. Visitors are not allowed on the Nicobar islands.

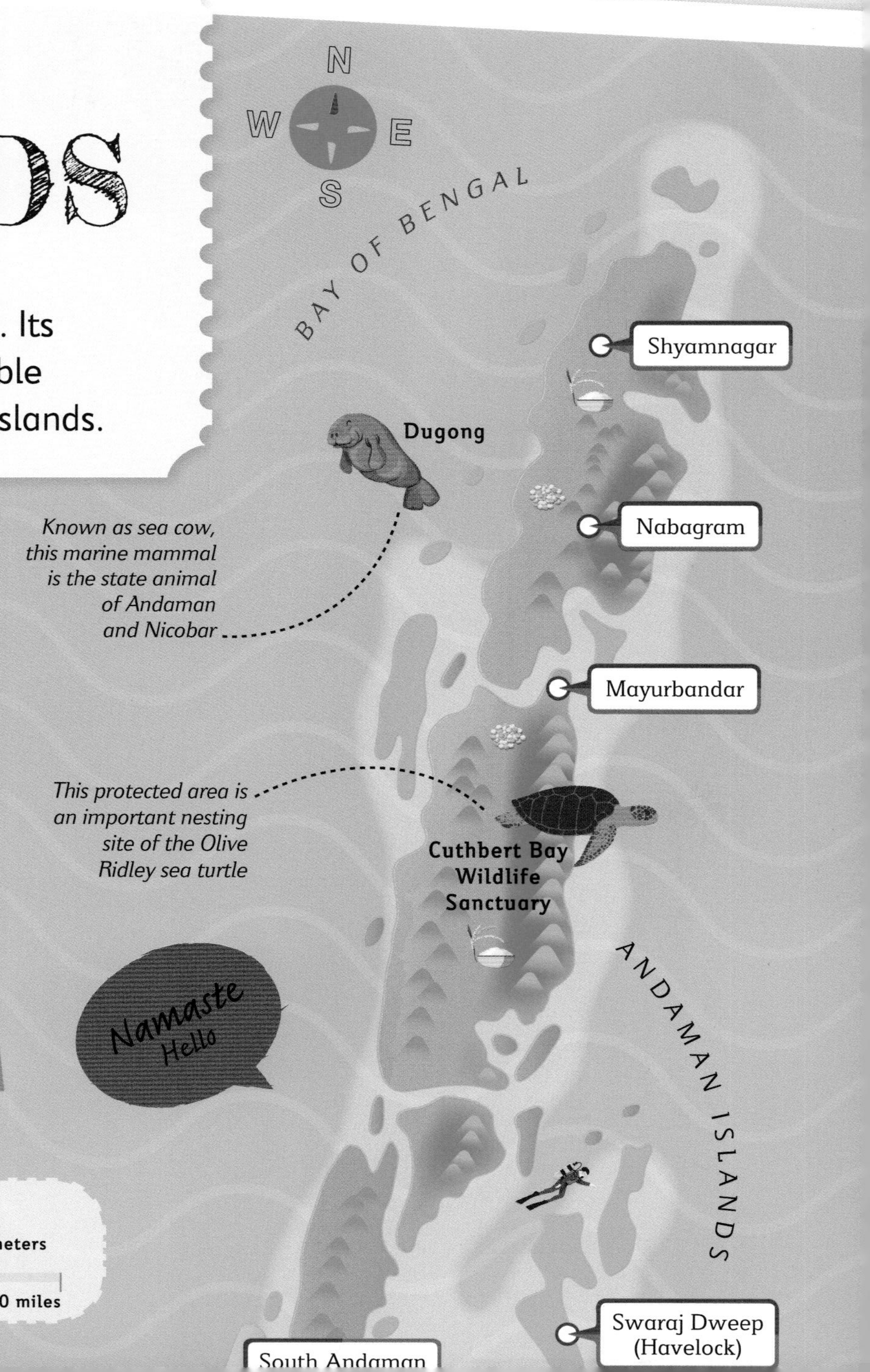

Shyamnagar

Nabagram

Mayurbandar

Swaraj Dweep (Havelock)

Dugong

Known as sea cow, this marine mammal is the state animal of Andaman and Nicobar

Cuthbert Bay Wildlife Sanctuary

This protected area is an important nesting site of the Olive Ridley sea turtle

N E S W

BAY OF BENGAL

ANDAMAN ISLANDS

South Andaman

Namaste
Hello

Radhanagar Beach

SCALE

0   20 kilometers

0   20 miles

Beaches

The archipelago is known for its pristine beaches, such as Radhanagar, Butler Bay, and Beach No. 5. Their turquoise water and exquisite white sand make for a picturesque landscape.

KEY

PRODUCE
Rice   Coconut
Oilseeds

ACTIVITIES
Snorkeling

Black-naped Oriole

Cellular Jail
This colonial prison, located in Port Blair, was constructed by the British in 1906. The jail gets its name from individual cells meant for solitary confinement.

Mount Harriet National Park
This national park in the South Andaman island supports remarkable biodiversity, such as the Andaman cobra and the black-naped oriole.

Shaheed Dweep (Neill)

Port Blair

Wandoor

Mahatma Gandhi Marine National Park
This marine park near Wandoor comprises 15 islands and many islets

Vandanalu
Hello

SCALE

0   25 kilometers

0   25 miles

N I C O B A R   I S L A N D S

The state tree is native to the island group

Andaman Padauk

Car Nicobar

Indigenous tribes
The islands are inhabited by six aboriginal tribes, such as Shompen and Jarawa. Most of them choose to live away from contact with outsiders. Their numbers have drastically reduced as a result of incessant immigration and loss of land.

Jarawa tribe

CULTURE

The country's geographical and cultural diversity have influenced its art forms. Most of these, from music and dance to theater and literature, have been around for hundreds of years.

MUSIC

Music has always been an important part of India's rituals and celebrations. The country's classical music tradition goes back thousands of years and has two branches, Hindustani and Carnatic. Each region also has its own treasury of folk songs.

AMIR KHUSROW

Known as the father of Qawwali, or devotional Sufi songs, Khusrow's music was based on the Sufi thought that union with God is achievable through prayers, regardless of religion or status.

Carnatic music
South India's classical music is based on raga (melody) and tala (rhythm). Compositions are called *kriti*, which are devotional in nature and feature instruments such as the flute, veena, and ghatam.

Hindustani music
Northern India's classical music form is believed to have originated around the 13th century. Musicians are separated into social organizations called *gharanas*, based on their apprenticeship and style.

Folk music
The diverse cultures in India have given birth to a range of rustic music traditions that mark special occasions such as festivals and new seasons. Each state has their own style, such as Pandavani from Chhattisgarh and Tappa from Punjab.

Modern Indian music
With the advent of the British in India, some western instruments such as clarinet and violin were incorporated into Indian music. The teaching of music was institutionalized and became accessible to more people.

DANCE

It is difficult to pinpoint when dance originated, but it has always been a form to express emotions. Dance is divided into folk and classical. The classical, or trained form, was performed in temples and in royal courts, while folk dance was a means to celebrate special occasions, such as festivals, marriages, and birth.

RUKMINI DEVI ARUNDALE

This dancer promoted Bharatanatyam, traditionally performed by devadasis, to remove the stigma attached to it. Twice nominated to the Rajya Sabha, Arundale was even invited to be the presidential candidate in 1977.

Kathak
The only classical dance from north India, it originated in the 16th–17th century.

Bharatanatyam
This classical form of temple dance from Tamil Nadu is more than 2,000 years old.

Odissi
This dance was traditionally performed to worship Lord Jagannath.

Manipuri
This devotional dance usually narrates episodes of Lord Krishna's separation from Radha.

Dandiya
This energetic folk dance from Gujarat is accompanied by rhythmic beating of batons.

THEATER

India has a rich history of performing dramas on stage, with the first plays dating back to the 2nd century BCE. Sage Bharata Muni, known as the father of theater, wrote the *Natyasastra*, an important study on dramatic arts.

Every state has its own form of folk theater such as Jatra from West Bengal, Nautanki from Uttar Pradesh, Ramman from Uttarakhand, and Bhavai from Gujarat.

Kathakali
Episodes from the epics are enacted in this dance-drama, which usually end with the destruction of a demon.

Tamasha
This folk form from Maharashtra is a combination of theater, singing, and dancing.

Yakshagana
This dance-drama from Karnataka is highly stylized and known for its elaborate costume and makeup.

CINEMA

The Indian film industry covers a wide gamut of languages—Hindi, Kannada, Konkani, Telugu, Malayam, Bengali, Marathi, and Tamil. Many Indian films have larger-than-life actors and plots, and elaborate sets.

DID YOU KNOW?

Kisan Kanya (1937), directed by Moti B. Gidwani, was India's first color talking movie.

DADASAHEB PHALKE
Regarded as the father of Indian cinema, Phalke was the director and producer of the first Indian feature film, Raja Harishchandra (1913).

DEVIKA RANI
Devika Rani was one of Hindi cinema's first successful actresses and is often referred to as the "first lady of the Indian screen." She was also the first recipient of the Dadasaheb Phalke Award, Indian cinema's highest award.

LITERATURE

Although the dictionary meaning of literature is "written work," the term covers works of fiction, poetry, drama, and religious texts. Indian literature evolved over time, from ancient philosophical texts to modern prose and poetry, reflecting the country's changing sociopolitical landscape.

DID YOU KNOW?

Many English words, such as summer, wheel, and nose, have Sanskrit roots.

PREMCHAND
A writer of Hindi and Urdu fiction, Premchand wrote as many as 250 stories and novels. His writings often criticized social evils. Some of his famous works, such as Godaan and Shatranj ke Khilari, have been adapted into films.

RABINDRANATH TAGORE
A prolific writer, poet, and artist, Rabindranath Tagore's writings left a deep impression on Indian literature and culture. He was the first Indian to win the Nobel Prize for Literature, in 1913.

PUDUCHERRY

This union territory is made up of four former French colonies of India, spread across three states—Mahe in Kerala, Yanam in Andhra Pradesh, and Karaikal and Puducherry in Tamil Nadu. The capital, Puducherry, still holds a distinct colonial flavor, with many streets and mansions retaining their French names.

KEY
PRODUCE
Rice
Sugarcane

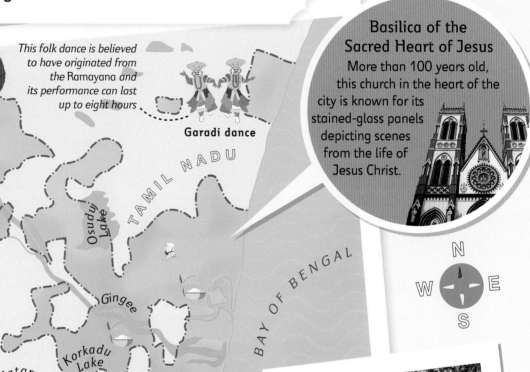

Vanakkam
Hello

This folk dance is believed to have originated from the *Ramayana* and its performance can last up to eight hours

Garadi dance

TAMIL NADU

Osudu Lake

Gingee

Korkadu Lake

Malataru

Bahour Lake

Thenpennai

BAY OF BENGAL

Basilica of the Sacred Heart of Jesus
More than 100 years old, this church in the heart of the city is known for its stained-glass panels depicting scenes from the life of Jesus Christ.

N
W   E
S

SCALE
0   5 kilometers
0   5 miles

French architecture

Auroville
A township aiming to bring people from different faiths and nationalities together, Auroville was founded on the principles of philosopher Sri Aurbindo Ghose. The compound has a spherical meditation chamber called Matrimandir.

White Town
One of Puducherry's distinct sectors, White Town retains its French heritage. It is known for its gray and yellow buildings, boulevards, and French cafés. Laid out in a grid pattern, the streets of the town cut across each other at right angles.

Kolkali dance

Dances
Different islands have their own folk dances, such as Parichakkali, Lava, and Kolkali. These dances form an integral part of marriages and festivities.

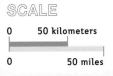

SCALE

0	50 kilometers
0	50 miles

KEY

ACTIVTIES
- Scuba diving
- Fisheries

Namaskaram
Hello

Coral reefs
Lakshadweep is an archipelago of 36 atolls—ring-shaped coral reef formations—that contain more than 90 varieties of corals.

Kadmat

Agatti

Kavaratti

Kalpeni

The capital has 52 mosques, Ujra being the most popular

Ujra Mosque

ARABIAN SEA

Corals

All islands in the archipelago have a lagoon

Lagoon

Minicoy

INDIAN OCEAN

N W E S

Beach in Minicoy

LAKSHADWEEP

An archipelago of 36 islands located in the Arabian Sea, southwest of the Kerala coast, Lakshadweep is the country's smallest union territory. Government permits are required to visit the islands in order to protect the region's natural ecosystem.

Minicoy Island
The southernmost island of the archipelago, Minicoy has a beautiful lagoon and stretch of mangroves along its shores.

KEY

PRODUCE
- Rice
- Tea
- Coconut
- Rubber

MINERALS
- Bauxite
- China Clay
- Limestone
- Quartz
- Silica
- Sillimanite

Sadya

A traditional vegetarian feast, it is served on a banana leaf and can have up to 28 different dishes at a time.

SCALE

0 — 25 kilometers

0 — 25 miles

Kerala backwaters

The scenic backwaters are a network of lagoons and lakes, connected through canals. Alappuzha, a city along the backwaters, is renowned for its houseboat cruises.

Houseboat cruise

These caves in Wayanad district have stone carvings believed to date back to the 7th century BCE

Wayanad

One of the last remaining rainforests in India, it is home to many animals, such as the lion-tailed macaque

Edakkal caves

Silent Valley National Park

NILGIRI HILLS

Kozhikode

Chaliyar

Kalaripayattu

Bharathapuzha

One of the oldest martial arts, it uses defined poses, gliding movements, and a variety of weapons

K A R N A T A K A

Valapattanam

Kannur

Mohiniyattam

Interpreted as the dance of Mohini, Vishnu's female form, Mohiniyattam's earliest text reference goes back to the 16th century

Namaskaram
Hello

Onam

The 10-day harvest festival marks the homecoming of Mahabali, the mythical, benevolent demon king. It is traditionally celebrated with flower *rangolis*, snake boat racing, elaborate feasts, and special dances.

At 8,842 ft (2,695m), this is the highest peak in the Western Ghats

There are more than 50 tea plantations in and around this hill station

The critically endangered Siberian crane migrates to this sanctuary, in Kottayam district, during summers

More than a thousand elephants can be found stomping their way through this forest

ANAMUDI

Munnar

CARDAMOM HILLS

Periyar Lake

Periyar Wildlife Sanctuary

The longest river in the state

Periyar

Kallada

Kumarakom Bird Sanctuary

The longest lake in the country

Kollam

Kochi

The Vembanad Backwater Lake

Alappuzha

Thiruvananthapuram

Kovalam

ARABIAN SEA

Thrissur

Chinese fishing nets

Built in 1568, this synagogue in Kochi is the country's oldest

Paradesi synagogue

Believed to have been introduced by Chinese explorers in the 14th–15th century, these are now a familiar sight along Kochi's coast

Sree Padmanabhaswamy Temple

Dedicated to Sree Padmanabhaswamy, the guardian deity of the royal family of Travancore, this is one of the richest Hindu temples in the world.

Kathakali

Performed exclusively by men, this dance-drama is known for its elaborate costumes, headgear, and makeup.

KERALA

Nestled between the Western Ghats and the Arabian Sea, this verdant state is blessed with beautiful beaches, calm backwaters, misty hills, and fragrant tea gardens. Commercial crops, such as tea, coffee, and rubber, are a major source of income for the state. Kerala also holds the distinction of being India's most literate state.

GLOSSARY

aboriginals
Original or first-known inhabitants of a country

archipelago
Group of islands

badland
Area of land that is often dry, rocky, and difficult to access

basalt
Commonly found dark volcanic rock

capital
A country or state's most important city that serves as the seat of the government

conifer
Evergreen trees with needlelike leaves that do not shed their leaves in winter

continent
Seven large areas of land that the world is divided into: Africa, Antarctica, Asia, Australia, Europe, North America, and South America

coral reefs
Rocklike structure formed by corals in the warm waters along tropical coasts. Many sea creatures live around coral reefs

country
A geographical area of land that is governed by the same leaders

dam
A concrete structure built to control the flow of a river, store water, and generate hydro-electricity

de facto
Something that exists and is accepted, but is not legally recognized

de jure
Something that is legally recognized

delta
Flat land formed from material deposited by a river around the area where it enters the sea or flows into a lake

desert
Dry region that gets 10 in (25 cm) or less of rainfall in a year. Deserts can be hot or cold. Only a few animals and plants are able to live in desert areas

endangered
A species of plant or animal with only a few living members left and on the verge of extinction

fertile land
Land where the soil is particularly good for growing crops

fossil
Remains or shape of a prehistoric plant or animal that has been preserved in rock

glacier
Huge, thick sheet of ice moving very slowly, either down the side of a mountain or over an area of land. Glaciers help to shape and form the landscape

gulf
Large area of sea that is almost enclosed by land, such as the Gulf of Mexico

hemisphere
Half of the earth, divided by the equator, or 0° latitude

island
Piece of land that has water all around it.
Islands occur in oceans, seas, lakes, and rivers

lagoon
A body of water with an opening into the sea

lake
Large body of water surrounded by land

latitude
Imaginary lines that run east to west across maps of the Earth

longitude
Imaginary lines that run from north to south across maps of the Earth

mangrove
Trees that grow in salt water

mine
Place where naturally occurring resources (such as coal) and gemstones are dug out of the ground

monsoon
Strong wind that blows across south and Southeast Asia. It changes direction as the seasons change, causing heavy rain

mountain
Area of land that rises up much higher

than the land around it to form a peak at the top

national park
Area of countryside that has been preserved in its natural state by the government of a country to protect the ecology

ocean
Very large sea. There are five oceans the world: Pacific Ocean, Atlantic Ocean, Indian Ocean, Arctic Ocean, and Southern Ocean

peninsula
Strip of land that is surrounded by water on three sides

plain
Area of flat, open land with very few trees. Plains are often covered with grass

plateau
Large area of high, flat land

population
Total number of people living in a given area of land

port
Town or city on the coast with a harbor, where boats and ships can be anchored

ravine
A deep, narrow valley

reservoir
Large natural or artificial lake where water is collected and stored

river
Large natural stream of water flowing in a definite course and draining into the sea

sanctuary
A nature reserve to protect one or more species

sea
Large body of salt water. Seas (including oceans) cover most of the Earth's surface

sediment
Tiny particles of mud and rock

species
Distinct group of animals or plants that share similar features

swamp
A wetland submerged in water

temperate
Climate characterized by mild temperatures

terrain
Area of land, usually with a particular feature, such as mountains, valleys, plateaus, or grassy plains

tribe
Group of people who share the same culture and history. It usually refers to people who live together in traditional communities, far from cities and towns

tributary
Smaller streams of water that flow into a river

tropical
Conditions found in areas near the Equator. Tropical weather is very hot and wet

union territory
An administrative division of land in India that is governed by the central government

valley
Low area of land between hills or mountains

vegetation
Type of plants found in an area of land

volcano
Mountain or hill that has a crater at the top through which hot lava may erupt

wetland
Land with wet, spongy soil, such as a marsh or swamp. Many animals and plants live only in wetland

INDEX

CREDITS

The publisher would like to thank the following people for their assistance in the preparation of this book: Alka Thakur for her help with the conceptualization; Priyanka Kharbanda and Rishi Bryan for editorial support; Ayushi Thapliyal for fact checking; Ashutosh Ranjan Bharti for cartographic assistance.

Picture Credits:
The publisher would like to thank the following for their kind permission to reproduce their photographs:

(Key: a-above; b-below/bottom; c-center; f-far; l-left; r-right; t-top)

10 Dreamstime.com: Soulart2012 (c, cb, bc). **11 Dreamstime.com:** EPhotocorp (br); Mdsindia (cr). **14 Dreamstime.com:** Gigisomplak (c/Crumple white paper, bl/Crumple white paper); Soulart2012 (c, bl); Leung Cho Pan (c/White crumple paper, bl/White crumple paper); Rudra Narayan Mitra / mitrarudra (c/Tiger hill); Fabio Lamanna (bl/ Rishikesh). **15 Dreamstime.com:** Gigisomplak (tr/Crumple white paper, cr/Crumple white paper, bl/Crumple white paper); Soulart2012 (tr, cr, bl); Leung Cho Pan (tr/White crumple paper, cr/White crumple paper, bl/White crumple paper); Diego Grandi (tr/Agra Fort); Odua (cr/Indian snack); Michael Smith (bl/Mustard). **16 Dreamstime.com:** Zaneta Cichawa (c); Phuongphoto (bl). **17 Dreamstime.com:** Irabel8 (bc); Narongc / narongcp (cr); Josef Skacel (tl). **18 Dorling Kindersley:** Neha Ahuja (bc). **Dreamstime.com:** Mircea Costina / Mirceax (c); Shailesh Nanal (br). **19 123RF.com:** PhotosIndia.com LLC (br). **Dreamstime.com:** Andrey Armyagov (tr). **20 Dreamstime.com:** Max5128 (br); Michael Smith (bc). **21 Dreamstime.com:** Vadim Chugaev (bc); Worasakc (bl); Wallixx (br). **22 Dreamstime.com:** Yogesh D (bc); S4sanchita (db). **Fotolia:** Ivan Kmit (tr). **23 123RF.com:** Raushan Singh (tc). **Dreamstime.com:** Kakoli Dey (da); Harshvardhan (crb). Nitish A: (cr). **24 Dorling Kindersley:** Saloni Singh / Prarthana (d). **Dreamstime.com:** Burt Johnson (bl); Saiko3p (c). **25 123RF.com:** Espies (c). **Dreamstime.com:** Elena Odareeva (tl); Sandesh Patil (br). **26 123RF.com:** Saiko3p (tr). **Dreamstime.com:** Anizza (db); Saiko3p (br). **27 Dreamstime.com:** Steve Allen (bc); Nigel Spiers (tr); Jeremy Richards (d). **30 Shreeram Deshpande. Dreamstime.com:** Iishwa (bc). **31 Dorling Kindersley:** Ayushi Thapliyal (tl/ Chikankari). **Dreamstime.com:** Euriico (cr); Burt Johnson (tc); Javarman (br). **32 Dreamstime.com:** Unissunil (tr). **36 Dreamstime.com:** Gigisomplak (da/Crumple white paper, bl/Crumple white paper); Soulart2012 (da, bl); Leung Cho Pan (da/White crumple paper, bl/White crumple paper, crb/White crumple paper); Saiko3p (da/Amer Fort); Parin Parmar (bl/Velaneshwar Beach); Dmitry Rukhlenko (crb/Thar Desert). **37 Dreamstime.com:** Gigisomplak (tr/Crumple white paper, br/Crumple white paper); Soulart2012 (tr, br); Leung Cho Pan (tr/White crumple paper, br/White crumple paper); Radiokafka (tr/Movie Poster); Gaurav Masand (br/ Rann of Kutch). **38 Dorling Kindersley:** Devika Awasthi (db). **Dreamstime.com:** Meinzahn (bc). **39 Dorling Kindersley:** Priyal Mote (tc). **Dreamstime.com:** Gaurav Masand (cra); Yurasova (br). **40 123RF.com:** Ivan Aleshin / ivan604 (crb). **Dreamstime.com:** Denicamp (bl); Kunal Sehrawat (c); Aliaksandr Mazurkevich (br). **41 Dorling Kindersley:** Devika Awasthi (tr). **Dreamstime.com:** Kailash Kumar (bc). **44 Dreamstime.com:** Rahul Barad (crb);

Kshishtof (tr). **45 Dreamstime.com:** Denicamp (cr); Homydesign (tr); Chandan Kumar (crb); Aleksandr Ugorenkov (tr/Bamboo mat). **Pixabay:** Pexels (tr/Crafts). **46-47 Dreamstime.com:** EPhotocorp (tc/Thalipith); Stock Image Factory (tc); Stock Image Factory (tc/Solkadhi). **47 123RF.com:** Anna ART **(b). Dreamstime.com:** Jatin Chadha (crb); Saiko3p (cb). Rajrupa: (tr). **50 Dreamstime.com:** Rahul Sutar (tc). **51 Dreamstime.com:** 204474 (cr); Denis Vostrikov (bl); Mnf1974 (db). **56 Dreamstime.com:** Gigisomplak (da/Crumple white paper, cb/Crumple white paper); Soulart2012 (da, cb); Leung Cho Pan (da/White crumple paper, cb/White crumple paper); Ugeshkumar (da/Chambal); Johnnydevil (cb/Gwalior Fort). **57 Dreamstime.com:** Gigisomplak (tr/Crumple white paper, bl/Crumple white paper); Soulart2012 (tr, bl); Leung Cho Pan (tr/White crumple paper, bl/White crumple paper); Andrey Gudkov (tr/Wild tiger); Samrat35 (bl/Tribal People). **58 Dreamstime.com:** Arindam Banerjee / Arindambanerjee (bl). **60 Dreamstime.com:** Soulart2012 (da, d, db). **62 Dreamstime.com:** Strahil Dimitrov (bl); Ksumano (c). **63 123RF.com:** Venkatramaiah Gidda (bl/Statuette). **Dreamstime.com:** Tarun Bhatia (db); Samrat35 (tr); Dario Lo Presti (bl); Gulrez K (bl/Mask & Bugle). **66 Dreamstime.com:** Gigisomplak (db/Crumple white paper, br/Crumple white paper); Soulart2012 (db, br); Leung Cho Pan (db/White crumple paper, br/White crumple paper); Samrat35 (db/Hornbill Festival); Elena Odareeva (br/Bamboo basket). **67 Dreamstime.com:** Gigisomplak (tc/Crumple white paper, c/Crumple white paper, br/Crumple white paper); Soulart2012 (tc, c, br); Leung Cho Pan (tc/White crumple paper, c/White crumple paper, br/White crumple paper); Steven Prorak (tc/Tea Plantation); Tshongang (c/Elephant); Hbh (br/Brahmaputra River). **68 Dreamstime.com:** Daawar15 (db); Amit Rane (tr); Joe Ravi (crb); Lambalmayum Kishorjit (bl); Mohak Gosavi (br). **69 Dreamstime.com:** Veeramani A (tl); Buddha13 (tr); Anuradha D Agrawal (d); Rudra Narayan Mitra (cr). **70 Dorling Kindersley:** Cotswold Wildlife Park (bl). **Dreamstime.com:** Manash Pratim Dutta (d); Tenzxwolve (tr). **71 Dreamstime.com:** Ananta Basumatary (da); David Talukdar (tl); Samrat35 (tl/Arts and Crafts); Demidoff (tl/ Mask); EPhotocorp (cra). **72 Dreamstime.com:** Aliaksandr Mazurkevich (cra); Neelamkakotymazumdar (d); Nilanjan Bhattacharya / Neelsky (bl). **73 123RF.com:** Prashansa Gurung (db). **Dreamstime.com:** Dwnld777 (bc); David Talukdar (cra). **74 Dorling Kindersley:** Wildlife Heritage Foundation, Kent, UK (da). **Dreamstime.com:** Buddha13 (crb); Aliaksandr Mazurkevich (tr). **75 123RF.com:** Rupa Ghosh (tr). **Dreamstime.com:** Donyanedomam (d); Ravsingh (crb). **78 123RF.com:** Suwatchai pluemruetai (da). **Dreamstime.com:** Lambalmayum Kishorjit (tr); B R Ramana Reddi (br). **79 Dreamstime.com:** Watchara Manusnanta (tr); Ppatty (br); Winai Tepsuttinun (br/Bamboo basket). **Getty Images:** IndiaPictures / UIG (d). **80 Dorling Kindersley:** Colin Keates / Natural History Museum, London (ca). **82 Dorling Kindersley:** Christopher Pillitz. **Dreamstime.com:** Nilanjan Bhattacharya (crb/Copper mines); Soulart2012 (da, crb, bl); Leung Cho Pan (da/White crumple paper., crb/White crumple paper., bl/White crumple paper.); Gigisomplak (da/Crumple white paper, crb/Crumple white paper, Crumple white paper); Saiko3p (da/Mahabodhi Temple). **83 Dreamstime.com:** Gigisomplak (crb/Crumple white paper); Soulart2012; Leung Cho Pan (White crumple paper.); Wichits (crb). **84 Dreamstime.com:** Kumar7075 (d).

85 Dreamstime.com: Samrat35 (tl); Samrat35 (cr). **Getty Images:** NurPhoto (db). **86 Dreamstime.com:** Leslie Clary (tr); Monica Furlong (d); Donyanedomam (c); EPhotocorp (db); Ganesh4photolife (db); Saiko3p (bl). **87 123RF.com:** Dinodia (da); Rupa Ghosh (tc); Saiko3p (d). **Dreamstime.com:** Arun Bhargava (cra); Samrat35 (tl); Parthkumar Bhatt (crb); Mdsindia (db). **88 123RF.com:** Norman Kin Hang Chan (bc); Dinodia (tc). **Dreamstime.com:** Oleg Ivanov (d); Rudra Narayan Mitra (crb). **89 123RF.com:** Alexandr Mychko (db). **Dreamstime.com:** Kiramogilenskikh (cr); Thomrutherford (br); Boris Ryzhkov (bl). **90 Dreamstime.com:** Nilanjan Bhattacharya (bc); Nazrul Islam (d); Kailash Kumar (tr). **91 Dreamstime.com:** Nilanjan Bhattacharya (bl); David Evison (tl); Kaushik Haldar (tr). **94 Dreamstime.com:** Tapas1978 (d). **95 123RF.com:** Beauty Pandit (bl). **Dreamstime.com:** Parthkumar Bhatt (crb); Picstudio (br). **98 Dreamstime.com:** Gigisomplak (d/Crumple white paper, bl/Crumple white paper); Soulart2012 (d, bl); Leung Cho Pan (d/White crumple paper, bl/White crumple paper); Raimond Klavins (d/Palm trees); Zafar Ibrahim (bl/Saraswati veena). **99 Dreamstime.com:** Gigisomplak (tr/Crumple white paper, c/Crumple white paper, bl/Crumple white paper); Soulart2012 (tr, c, bl); Leung Cho Pan (tr/White crumple paper, c/White crumple paper, bl/White crumple paper); Mohamed Kasim Naufal (tr/Emerald Lake); Rajesh K N (c/Snake Boat); Iuliia Kryzhevska (bl/Sri Ranganathaswamy Temple). **100 Dreamstime.com:** Marina Pissarova (bc). **101 Dorling Kindersley:** Rupa Rao (da). **Dreamstime.com:** Mnsanthoshkumar (bc); Saiko3p (br). **104 Dreamstime.com:** Truptimayee Maharana (cra); Denis Vostrikov (br). **105 Dorling Kindersley:** Prarthana (cra). **Dreamstime.com:** Kunal Sehrawat (da). **108 Dreamstime.com:** Soulart2012 (db, cb, crb, bl, bc, br). **109 Dreamstime.com:** Soulart2012 (db, cb, crb, bl, bc, br). **110 Dorling Kindersley:** Dharini (bc). **Dreamstime.com:** Maria1986nyc (d). **111 Dreamstime.com:** Steve Allen (tr); Gamutstockimagespvtltd (tl); Vladimir Zhuravlev (c); Oleg Ivanov (br). **114 Dreamstime.com:** Wallixx (c). **115 Dreamstime.com:** Vasyl Helevachuk (tr); Jayk67 (tc). **Getty Images:** Thierry Falise / LightRocket (db). **116 Dreamstime.com:** Soulart2012 (bl, bc, bc/Brochure, bc/Tri fold brochure, br). **117 Dreamstime.com:** Soulart2012 (tr, cra, cra/Brochure). **118 Dreamstime.com:** Ajay Bhaskar (bl); Denis Vostrikov (cra); Beat Germann (crb). **119 Dreamstime.com:** John Anderson (tr/Soft corals); Aji Jayachandran (tl); Fatema7864 (crb); Tententenn (tr); Valentyna Chukhlyebova (tr/Red Coral); Dimjul (tr/Sea coral); Natee Srisuk (tr/Red Coral on white). **120 123RF.com:** Dinodia (bc). **Dreamstime.com:** Mnsanthoshkumar (db); Vladimir Zhuravlev (tc). **121 Dreamstime.com:** Ivan Varyukhin (c); Zzvet (b)

All other images © Dorling Kindersley

For further information see: www.**dk**images.com